To Harriet
God Bless
Linda Rudd Santin
11-20-2021

Love
Notes
TO GOD ...

Love Notes TO GOD ...

POETRY FROM A MENDED HEART:

A Year Long Journey into the
Depths of God's Love

LINDA RUDD SAUTER

Xulon Press
2301 Lucien Way #415
Maitland, FL 32751
407.339.4217
www.xulonpress.com

Paperback ISBN-13: 978-1-6628-0944-6

eBook ISBN-13: 978-1-6628-0945-3

Table of Contents

Introduction

Have you ever been faced with a life–changing disappointment that shattered your world of security leaving you frightened, depressed, feeling rejected and you said to yourself, "This is not how my life was supposed to be?"

Sometimes we find ourselves in a valley struggling to make it out, longing to be on the mountaintop, but that mountain seems so far away and so impossible to climb or maybe we are so far down in the valley that we can't even see our way out and wondering, is there an end in sight? Or will my heart ever be healed? Through the brokenness God draws us closer, strengthens us, and teaches how to totally trust Him. He only desires good for us, because He loves us so very much, but unforeseen circumstances can still happen. I know because I have been there.

As I open up my heart in the following story, I pray, it will give you a glimpse to see how God has created newness in my life. How He has given me deeper hope and to assure you He will do that for you as well.

God has always been here for me I truly believe that, there has never been a doubt, yet one day my life changed and I found myself all alone with an overwhelming fear of not knowing what to do. I dropped to my knees, weeping on my living room floor with feelings of emptiness and failure. As I prayed through a river of tears, it was in that moment my loving God assured me He was right there with me. He met me on my living room floor, but did not leave me there. I could feel His presence around me and I knew then He was the only one in life that I could truly count on. He would be my lifeline and my comforter, giving me courage to keep going.

I searched for every moment I could find to just run to Him to pray, read His Word and cry in His presence. I wanted to be there all the time. I wished the world would stop for a while, to just stop spinning. In the book of Psalms my Bible tells me, "As the deer pants for streams of water, so my soul pants for You, my God." In those moments that seemed like a lifetime I was so thirsty for God and in so much need of Him. I wanted to drink in all I could. I memorized Jeremiah 29:11. I read it over and over again, that God has a plan for me.

Have you ever had a friend who just knows your every thought? Someone you can tell them everything and it just feels right? Someone who you can sit with in the quiet nights, feeling their presence yet not have to say a word? God had always been my answer to what I needed. He was my truest friend.

Then one night I awoke and began to pray. I had quite often done this as it helped me get through a lot of sleepless nights. Nights with such a heavy weight of panic I could hardly breathe and I just had to pray to get to the next day. I hid most of my feelings. No one but God knew. And day after day I could feel Him making me stronger. But then on this night as I prayed I just felt I needed to get up and write down my prayer. As I wrote, I realized the words were in the form of a poem. The next day all that was on my mind was praising God and writing what I was thinking, and it appeared to be in the same form again. I can't explain it, but I know my life has taken a turn and I am not sure where God is leading me, but all I want to do is follow Him. I am thankful He has made Himself real to me and I cherish these moments in writing, Love Notes To God, Poetry From A Mended Heart. While I express my heart to Him, He reminds me I am loved and has shown me how to forgive as He forgives. I am so grateful for His constant companionship, His unconditional mercy and peace and His strength He gives day by day. I realized when there is an end there is always a new beginning.

If you have felt discouraged, hurt or lost, I hope I have been able to encourage you to keep looking up. I would like you to know, God is always faithful to meet us just where we are. In fact, He is always there first.

This devotional was meant to be a Year–Long daily meditation time or an addition to the reader's daily quiet time with God. In reading, Love Notes To God, Poetry From A Mended Heart, I pray you feel the love of God through the words. May you find new hope, peace and divine comfort in a closer relationship with our Savior. Please trust God to bring you through every situation because He is bigger than any problem we have. Turn to Him and He will see you through, that is His promise. And remember, He has a plan for you as well...

Blessings,
Linda Rudd Sauter

"For I know the plans I have for you," says the Lord. "They are plans for good and not for disaster, to give you a future and a hope." Jeremiah 29:11 (NLT)

Reference Scripture: "As the deer pants for streams of water, so my soul pants for You, my God." Psalm 42:1 (NIV)

January

January 1
In Loving Grace

Satisfy us in the morning with your steadfast love,
that we may rejoice and be glad all our days.
Psalm 90:14 (ESV)

Lord, I meet You as the morning sun rises in the sky.
For I need You every moment as each day passes by.

I will thank You no matter what this life shall bring.
And through all trials and triumphs, I'll humbly sing.

Lord, I praise You for Your peaceful and loving way,
You are more to me than any words could ever say.

My devotion and love will be forever given to You,
I trust Your steadfast hand will guide me through.

In loving grace one day, I'll bow before Your glory.
For You have written every page of my life story.

January 2
HAND IN HAND

I am able to do all things through Him who strengthens me.
Philippians 4:13 (HCSB)

Lord, my heart is overjoyed because I know You live.
The hope within me is steadfast because You forgive.

There is strength in knowing You can do all things,
My future and hope is whatever Your desire brings.

The days are happy walking with You hand in hand,
And my life is blessed because You have it planned.

Thank You, Lord, You're the awesome priceless One.
I give You praise for all the wonders You have done.

Living my days without You would be sad and bleak,
Father, You are the One in this life I will always seek.

January 3
SACRED MOMENTS LIKE THIS

Surely goodness and mercy shall follow me all the days of my life:
and I will dwell in the house of the LORD for ever.
Psalm 23:6 (KJV)

Holy Father, let me feel Your presence today,
In silence, I come alone just to kneel and pray.

While I rest in the shadow of this old oak tree,
I ponder Your goodness graciously given to me.

As raindrops fall sunrays slowly peak through,
Lord, I'm amazed of the beauty because of You.

Amongst the flowers, the paths lead to and fro,
The various trails I wonder where they will go.

The pond is peaceful now the storm has gone,
With the beautiful sight, I could stay till dawn.

Lord, I thank You for sacred moments like this.
Precious times with You I never want to miss.

January 4
NO REASON TO GIVE UP

Do you not know that in a race all the runners run,
but only one receives the prize? So run that you may obtain it.
1 Corinthians 9:24 (ESV)

Lord, my heart cries out to You again today.
As I devote my life, please guide Your way.

I run to You when trials consume my mind,
For in Your presence, peace is what I find.

I will listen for what You want me to hear,
As I wait for Your soft whisper in my ear.

You're my protector and my strong shield,
Lord, I have faith in You, my heart I yield.

Life is difficult with no answers in sight,
But there's no reason to give up the fight.

No matter what the past or future to be,
I'll trust You, Lord, and forever seek Thee.

January 5
YOU ARE MY GOD

I will sing unto the LORD as long as I live:
I will sing praise to my God while I have my being.
Psalm 104:33 (KJV)

You are my God of peace with devoted pure love,
Your presence is comforting, flowing from above.

You are my God of truth, joy and humbled grace,
I'm so thankful, Lord, as I kneel to seek Your face.

You are my God of plenty, providing every need.
As I journey through life, I will follow Your lead.

You are my God of hope as I rejoice all day long,
For within my heart, Lord, You've placed a song.

You are my God of salvation so worthy of praise,
I give You glory for Your Holy Name I will raise.

You are my God of mercy, far beyond measure,
You are my God of truth, my precious treasure.

January 6
WITH HEARTFELT TEARS

You, God, are my God, earnestly I seek you;
I thirst for you, my whole being longs for you ...
Psalm 63:1 (NIV)

Lord, in humble prayer I ask to draw me near,
For You are my closest friend I know so dear.

My soul smiles because Your Spirit is sweet,
Every day my heart longs to sit at Your feet.

You remove worries and burdensome fear,
I'm filled with peace because You are here.

I desire others to know Your goodness I see,
And to feel Your love that flows through me.

I thank You for tender mercy in all my years,
As I give You praise with my heartfelt tears.

January 7
THROUGH THE STORM

And the peace of God, which transcends all understanding,
will guard your hearts and your minds in Christ Jesus.
Philippians 4:7 (NIV)

With You, Lord, Your timing is never too late.
Through trials, I've learned it's best to wait.

As I quietly pray, uncertain what more to do,
In my heart, I know I must leave it with You.

I'm grateful even if life is tattered and torn,
I know You always protect through the storm.

As the enemy tries to hurt and tear us down,
Your mercy brings a smile instead of a frown.

While I trust You the troubles always cease,
I am thankful Your Word brings total peace.

I will praise You for every moment each day,
As I follow You, Lord, in walking Your way.

January 8
I Want to Be a Testimony

If any of you lacks wisdom, you should ask God, who gives generously to all without finding fault, and it will be given to you.
James 1:5 (NIV)

I give thanks, Lord, because I want You to know.
To tell of Your greatness because I love You so.

My heart is full of gladness only You can bring,
Praising You forever with joyful words I'll sing.

I want to be a testimony of Your peace and grace.
As I'm molded in Your time and appointed place.

I'm grateful for Your presence when trials begin,
For You bring renewed hope time and time again.

Let my life reflect Your light each breath I take,
And let my walk honor You in every step I make.

January 9
ENDLESS JOY

Ah, Lord God!
It is You who have made the heavens and the earth by Your great
power and by Your outstretched arm! Nothing is too hard for You.
Jeremiah 32:17 (ESV)

Lord, Your amazing beauty is in every sunrise,
I praise You for the hues of magnificent skies.

I feel Your presence in quiet times with You,
Lord, I pray You'll show me what I am to do.

I know of Your love and promise to be near,
In my heart, Your soft whisper I wait to hear.

Your endless joy is beauty that grace brings,
As I meditate on You, Lord, my heart sings.

My strength and peace comes in Your name.
Your Word tells You will always be the same.

All things are possible when in You we believe.
In Your time, Lord, as we trust, we will receive.

January 10
I Bow to Worship

*"All mankind will come to worship Me from one New Moon
to another and from one Sabbath to another,"
says the LORD.
Isaiah 66:23 (HCSB)*

Heavenly Father, I'm praying You draw me near,
While in the quiet moonlight, I'm waiting to hear.

I need You by my side each minute of every day,
I will remain still in listening for what You say.

All the many times You have carried me through,
I yearn for more moments, I can spend with You.

Lord, in all brokenness, You are the healer of life.
You are with us faithfully, through all the strife.

There is no one who cares in loving ways You do,
I bow to worship, Lord, for making hearts new.

January 11
THIS HUMBLE PRAYER

Jesus said to him, "If you can believe,
all things are possible to him who believes."
Mark 9:23 (NKJV)

Lord, I ask Your blessings for lost ones today,
They need You to help them walk on their way.

There are times when I find it difficult to pray,
But You see my heart and what I want to say.

Lord, I ask for those who need a healing touch.
And others who seek Your presence so much.

Your hand gives hope and strength to carry on,
You're the Savior of the world, God's only Son.

I humbly give praise and glory to Your name,
For it is Your love I will always proclaim.

Lord, I trust You've heard this humble prayer,
I thank You for listening, for I know You care.

January 12
Let My Life Be a Praise Song

Let everything that has breath praise the LORD!
Psalm 150:6 (NKJV)

Lord, on my journey I've always felt Your precious love.
My life is a glory story because of You I can rise above.

Your promises give peace, I am happy all the day long.
I worship You, Lord, for Your strength keeps me strong.

Every morning I await to be alone with You when I rise,
I imagine Your face while I look up to beautiful skies.

Your presence is like a waterfall refreshing as I thirst,
With every trial I go through, I know You're there first.

Lord, let my life be a praise song written just for You.
Thank You for walking with me, making each day new.

January 13
ASHES FOR BEAUTY

In his kindness God called you to share in his eternal glory by means of Christ Jesus. So after you have suffered a little while, he will restore, support, and strengthen you, and he will place you on a firm foundation.
1 Peter 5:10 (NLT)

Lord, you give rich blessings in all things You display,
The beauty of this life is woven into every single day.

I will give praise on this journey as all honor is due,
As You lead me on Your path growing closer to You.

Help me see Your will, Lord, as I cling to Your hope,
Alone with You brings peace, giving strength to cope.

You're my strong shield; I know in my heart for sure.
I ask You, Lord, to refine me, giving joy as I endure.

Going through times of trial may be for my own good,
As You replace ashes for beauty as only You could.

January 14
A PLAN FROM THE BEGINNING

In him we have obtained an inheritance, having been predestined according to the purpose of him who works all things according to the counsel of his will.
Ephesians 1:11 (ESV)

Here I am God, I'm just praising and loving You,
I'll worship, Heavenly Father, for all that You do.

You faithfully provide all necessary things I need,
Through grace and mercy, my life is Yours to lead.

Worldly things are not at all what matters in life,
Living is about You as hearts are mended in strife.

God, You had a plan from the beginning of all time.
When our Savior came for souls, including mine.

Thank You for loving enough to sacrifice Your Son,
Because of Him, I have hope and eternity has won.

January 15
OPEN MY EYES

Don't neglect to do what is good and to share,
for God is pleased with such sacrifices.
Hebrews 13:16 (HCSB)

Lord, You have shown me joy in following Your way.
As I listen for Your voice, every time I kneel to pray.

Your presence embraces all things perfect and right,
Help me, Lord, to keep Your will totally in my sight.

Please open my eyes to see all those who are in need,
By doing whatever I can, even if just planting a seed.

Help me show Your love and mercy You always give,
It is truly my desire as long as I am destined to live.

When I reflect on Your grace and gift of eternal love,
Lord, I'm fulfilled because of Your peace from above.

January 16
THE MOST PERFECT BLESSING

He has made everything beautiful in its time. Also He has put
eternity in their hearts, except that no one can find out the
work that God does from beginning to end.
Ecclesiastes 3:11 (NKJV)

God, Your beauty amazes me in the early morning light,
And Your masterpiece is awesome as stars fill the night.

I see You as birds find treasures in tending their nest,
They carefully place items to make a home for her rest.

As butterflies visit flowers and all the fragrant things,
I hear soft music flow from tiny hummingbird wings.

Your presence is heard as waves splash on the shore.
As seashells wash back and forth we see even more.

You are heard in a child's laughter as the game is won,
Yet the most perfect blessing is Jesus Your Divine Son.

Thank You, Holy God, for giving Your mercy and grace.
And someday we can rejoice, for we will see Your face.

January 17
HOPE FOR EVERYTHING

Therefore He is also able to save to the uttermost those who come to God through Him, since He always lives to make intercession for them.
Hebrews 7:25 (NKJV)

Lord, You're my strength, my Rock on which I stand.
I'm trusting in Your promises as I hold to Your hand.

When we're hurt and feel we can't endure anymore,
You are always there to heal and faithfully restore.

Lord, my soul weeps for those falling to earthly sin.
And Yours must break as hearts lack belief within.

You gave up life for our undeserving souls to save,
I pray, all will accept Your priceless gift You gave.

You are hope for everything planned on our way,
As Your Spirit guides us each moment of the day.

January 18
Courage in Sharing

And we are confident that he hears us whenever we ask for anything that pleases him.
1 John 5:14 (NLT)

God, Your love is a treasure held deep within,
Your grace makes joy from the ashes of sin.

I am forever safe in Your gentle arms of rest.
Because You are with me, I am truly blessed.

I want to thank You for Your awesome care.
Please grant wisdom as I seek You in prayer.

Give me courage in sharing with those I see,
For my heart is bursting with praise for Thee.

God, I ask to be guided by Your shining light,
Please strengthen me by day and every night.

One day may I hear You whisper, "Well done,"
As I strive to live my life honoring Your Son.

January 19
AN OBEDIENT HEART

"Give, and it will be given to you. Good measure, pressed down,
shaken together, running over, will be put into your lap.
For with the measure you use it will be measured back to you."
Luke 6:38 (ESV)

As I pray, Lord, I'm reminded of needs around me today,
Please allow Your Spirit to bear guidance with no delay.

Nothing is more important than seeking Your loving face,
As I am truly blessed and covered by Your endless grace.

In Your abundance of mercy, please allow my eyes to see,
Show me how to reach others as I joyfully glorify Thee.

Teach me to share with a pure heart all in good measure.
For Your Word and promise is my only secure treasure.

Give me an obedient heart to always honor in what I do,
While I trust in Your mighty power to carry me through.

January 20
THE ONLY PATH TO PEACE

Blessed is a person who finds wisdom. And one who obtains understanding.
Proverbs 3:13 (NASB)

Lord, why do people hurt others in the way they do?
Why is it they fail to love unconditionally like You?

Why is so much hate and deceit in this world today?
Why are aborted babies never given the right to say?

Why are some unfaithful with the vows they forget?
Why are many chained to the sin they will regret?

Why do people live in darkness by day and night?
Why are they blinded, not willing to see Your light?

Why do they cling to strongholds that never cease?
Lord, I pray they see You are the only path to peace.

January 21
FAVOR THROUGH DIVINE EYES

For You, LORD, bless the righteous one;
You surround him with favor like a shield.
Psalm 5:12 (HCSB)

In this quiet, I sense Your presence within my heart.
I totally surrender my life to You, Lord, in every part.

I'm thankful You're here because I need You so much,
To just feel the overflowing joy of Your healing touch.

I have shared happiness and struggles with shed tears,
Through the past, You've never left me in all the years.

In brokenness, You've given favor through divine eyes,
And You have protected me from all the enemy's lies.

Thank You, Lord, for holding me in Your strong hands.
My true hope is to live guided by Your desired plans.

January 22
The Love of My Life

"And you shall love the LORD your God with all your heart,
with all your soul, with all your mind, and with all your strength."
Mark 12:30 (NKJV)

Lord, the moment I met You our hearts lovingly embraced,
Our souls were intertwined with joy and the past erased.

As my love grows for You, the memories I value each day,
I cherish the time together with happiness along my way.

You are the only One who understands my heart the best.
By day You hear my prayers and nights You give me rest.

Love is meant for a lifetime and devotion to always stay,
For nothing takes the place or no one should steal away.

I praise You, Lord, for grace because You are God's Son,
You are the love of my life and always will be the One.

January 23
IN YOUR PRESENCE I FIND JOY

"For where your treasure is, there will your heart be also."
Matthew 6:21 (KJV)

With You, Lord, I praise humbly until my soul overflows.
Your joy and peace have been planted where love grows.

When I rise in the morning, it's always You I long to see,
At night I'm at rest as I thank You for watching over me.

While I look back on life You always carried me through,
It is amazing how pain has vanished and I am made new.

Your Word is treasured in my heart through end of time,
For in Your presence, I find joy that will always be mine.

As I think of You, Lord, there aren't enough words to say,
You always know my thoughts every time I come to pray.

When my direction is uncertain and I seek where to go,
Your hand is always faithful for in time You let me know.

January 24
HELP ME HEAR YOUR WHISPER

Teach me to do Your will, for You are my God.
May Your gracious Spirit lead me on level ground.
Psalm 143:10 (HCSB)

Lord, You know my heart how I long to be with You.
I depend on Your strength daily to carry me through.

Guide me, Lord, to be patient as I listen for Your voice.
Often directions are unseen in making the right choice.

My desire is for Your Spirit flowing gently through me,
With all that I have, I want to glorify and honor Thee.

Your grace and peace You give refreshes from above,
As I rest in the beauty of Your endless, heavenly love.

As You speak to my heart to reflect Your divine will,
God, help me hear Your whisper as I learn to be still.

January 25
WHEN I CAN'T SEE THE END

"The Lord lives! Praise to my Rock!
My God, the Rock of my salvation, be exalted!"
2 Samuel 22:47 (NLT)

Lord, I'm grateful Your hope comforts when I call,
And how You cradle as my strength begins to fall.

In Your hands, I will commit everything that I do,
Please calm the storms for I desperately need You.

When I can't see the end, Lord, I'll still hold tight,
For no matter what, You've already won the fight.

Thank You, Lord, for Your love and endless peace.
And for Your Spirit that gives joy as burdens cease.

In all trials, You have always been with me there.
And on this journey I'm reminded how You care.

January 26
WINDOWS OF MY HEART

"Blessed are the pure in heart, for they will see God."
Matthew 5:8 (NIV)

Lord, please refine me as You search rooms of my heart.
Revealing to me all that needs to change in every part.

The clutter that causes fear tear down and sweep away,
Fill those areas with faith, love and joy I ask You today.

Lord, the things I do that aren't acceptable in Your eyes.
Please bring all those to surface and help me be wise.

Open windows of my heart flowing Your light through,
Allowing my life to be a blessing always to glorify You.

Lord, please speak into my spirit as You hold my hand,
Let my life give You honor in ways You have planned.

January 27
I'll Trust in You

Keep thy heart with all diligence; for out of it are the issues of life.
Proverbs 4:23 (KJV)

Lord, I thank You for all You mean to me I pray,
I will walk with You each moment of every day.

Help me to see things that really matter to You,
While I seek for Your wisdom in all that is true.

Erase thoughts You would not have me believe,
Only those of hope and mercy I want to receive.

I'll trust in You, Lord, please guide in Your will,
Help me take the time to listen and just be still.

I want to honor You with a heart that is clean,
Forever I praise You and close to You I'll lean.

January 28
EARLY MORNING PRAISE

But I will sing of your strength, in the morning I will sing of your love;
for you are my fortress, my refuge in times of trouble.
Psalm 59:16 (NIV)

Lord, I come this morning before the sun begins to rise,
Asking You to reveal what is pleasing within Your eyes.

As I walk along the path, trusting Your will for my life,
I'll thank You for Your peace as I endure all the strife.

Each day is a gift from You I'm grateful for Your grace,
And when I'm sad, You hold me close in Your embrace.

You whispered joy as I cling to Your promises for me.
My heart is humbled I'll always trust Your plans to be.

In early morning praise, I give my loving heart to Thee,
For Your endless blessings and mercies, every day I see.

January 29
EVERY DAY IS BLESSED

*Jesus said to him, "You shall love the LORD your God with
all your heart, with all your soul, and with all your mind."
Matthew 22:37 (NKJV)*

Every day I wait for those moments we can share,
I long to be together, Lord, when I kneel in prayer.

Every day I am with You I long for the time to last.
For I miss those precious memories as time is past.

Every day is uncertain whatever You have planned,
But You are my guide, and on Your Word I'll stand.

Every day is blessed, always given in a special way.
As You grant breakthroughs when in life we obey.

Every day Your goodness outshines the day before,
I'll praise You, Lord, because I love You even more.

January 30
THROUGH EVERY TRIAL

"You will know the truth, and the truth will set you free."
John 8:32 (HCSB)

Lord, Your presence comforts like a gentle spring rain.
It is amazing how You wash away sin and every stain.

Your love and truth go far beyond anything I can say.
Yet in this quiet place, I'm sure You hear when I pray.

How the thoughts of You, Lord, make my heart smile.
My soul has peace for You're here through every trial.

Living life with You gives happiness to each new day,
Even through the valley, You guide me along the way.

While I seek Your plans, Lord, I commit my life to You,
As You look into my heart, You can see my love is true.

January 31
LOVING EYES FROM ABOVE

*Behold, the eye of the LORD is on those who fear Him,
on those who hope in His mercy.*
Psalm 33:18 (NKJV)

Lord, in the quiet times with You all things I can share.
You understand my heart and see how very much I care.

You shine peace into my life in that special way You do,
I am thankful for all You've done bringing me through.

Trials cease when in Your presence I kneel at Your feet,
For I know the time I spend with You is always sweet.

I rest in You, Lord, for Your guidance, peace and love,
Please watch over with Your loving eyes from above.

I'm so unworthy of Your great blessings given to me,
You're my treasure and forever You will hold the key.

February

February 1
LET MY PRAISE HONOR YOU

I will praise the name of God with a song,
and will magnify him with thanksgiving.
Psalm 69:30 (ASV)

Thank You, Lord, for blessings and courage You give,
For mercy and abundant grace in this world, we live.

You are my best friend, so loving, amazing and kind.
You know every hurt and the thoughts on my mind.

You give peace and comfort more than I have known,
No matter what this life brings, I will never be alone.

You are my refuge and I lay my prayers at Your feet,
As I wait for the time, we will someday finally meet.

Let my praise honor You, Lord, as I worship this day,
May You be glorified with loving thoughts as I pray.

February 2
SCARS AND STRIPES

For he satisfies the longing soul,
and the hungry soul he fills with good things.
Psalm 107:9 (ESV)

Lord, when we are hurting, how do we measure the pain?
True peace comes only when we give to You every chain.

You took our burdens because You knew it wasn't a loss,
As You suffered the stripes and carried the heavy Cross.

In times of trial, Your presence will change who we are,
Because You came to remove our wounds and every scar.

Often we cannot see beyond darkness that masks the sky,
Yet Your light filters down as mercy comes from on high.

Your plan is shown each moment as You breathe new life,
For it is by Your power that removes discord and strife.

Lord, Your peace satisfies thirst from our searching soul,
As we remain close to You, Your grace makes us whole.

February 3
HOPE IN THIS LIFE AND AFTER

He came as a witness, to bear witness about the light,
that all might believe through him.
John 1:7 (ESV)

On this journey, Lord, You give peace for everyday I see,
While at the end, I know You will be in eternity with me.

Along this path, I will remain clinging tight to Your hand,
The promise of Heaven tells me You have life all planned.

Thank You for Your provisions and every beautiful sight.
As the brilliance of the sun reveals, Your glorious light.

Praise belongs to You, Lord, for hope in this life and after,
Each day with You is a time of grace and joyful laughter.

You mend our broken hearts, comforting all our sorrows,
Lord, yesterdays are gone, but You hold our tomorrows.

February 4
FATHERLY LOVE

*As a father has compassion on his children,
so the LORD has compassion on those who fear Him.
Psalm 103:13 (HCSB)*

Kneeling in Your presence, Lord, You comfort me,
When I am with You I know You hear every plea.

Lord, allow me a loyal and tender heart like You,
Let me have a humble spirit, committed and true.

My devotion will always be Yours as long as I live,
I am very grateful because of everything You give.

Your blessings are free and granted from above,
As You faithfully provide precious fatherly love.

Lord, I cannot find enough words of praise to say,
Yet You see how I long to be with You each day.

February 5
STRENGTH EACH DAY

"Surely God is my salvation; I will trust and not be afraid.
The LORD himself, is my strength and my defense;
he has become my salvation."
Isaiah 12:2 (NIV)

Lord, I am trusting, I humbly give You all my heart.
As I joyfully seek Your presence never to be apart.

I lift my hands in worship, waiting on what's in store,
Please guide my path as I walk through every door.

You are the Comforter, giving me strength each day,
Lord, You hear my every thought even before I pray.

All life trials take time for the storms to move past,
Yet true promises in Your Word will always last.

Lord, I need You, my prayer is to live in Your will.
Thank You for peace in valleys and up every hill.

February 6
Teach Me, Holy Spirit

*But the Helper, the Holy Spirit, whom the Father will send
in My name, He will teach you all things and bring
to your remembrance all things that I said to you.*
John 14:26 (NKJV)

Lord, You have granted joy in times I've felt pain,
And rescued from every burden and every chain.

You cover with gentle peace and abundant hope,
With You, I always have strength enough to cope.

Teach me, Holy Spirit, as I draw wisdom from You,
Help to discern Your truth as I journey through.

Lord, I want to always be acceptable in Your sight.
To let go of earthly desires, led only by Your light.

As I walk with You, Your awesome goodness I see,
You are so wonderful, God, take free reign in me.

February 7
Never Too Late

But they that wait upon the LORD shall renew their strength;
they shall mount up with wings as eagles; they shall run, and
not be weary; and they shall walk, and not faint.
Isaiah 40:31 (KJV)

Heavenly Father, if ever we needed You it is now,
Our loved ones are waiting for answers somehow.

You hear concerns when lifted to you as we pray,
In silence we need You more than words can say.

I trust You, Lord, believing You can do all things.
As we lay worries at Your feet and praises I sing.

Hearts that seek Your touch please restore today,
Let our humble requests be heard without delay.

In prayer for healing and with patience we wait,
Thank You, Lord, for favor You are never too late.

February 8
LET YOUR WILL BE DONE

Now the Lord is the Spirit, and where the Spirit
of the Lord is, there is freedom.
2 Corinthians 3:17 (NIV)

Lord, thank You for peace that gently comforts me,
Please let Your Spirit shine brightly for all to see.

I've learned to let go waiting for Your open doors,
Not listening to my thoughts, but seeking Yours.

There is everlasting freedom in Your hope, I found,
I am redeemed and I stand on Your solid ground.

Lord, I pray to glorify You in everything I shall do,
Please guide me to be totally focused on only You.

As grace and joy flows from Your gracious hand,
Let Your will be done as You divinely planned.

February 9
A Stronghold to All That Are Weak

The LORD is my rock, and my fortress, and my deliverer;
my God, my strength, in whom I will trust; my buckler,
and the horn of my salvation, and my high tower.
Psalm 18:2 (KJV)

The ocean of pain strives to wash away my joy,
Yet I'm grateful, Lord, the enemy cannot destroy.

The storms are conquered by Your mighty hand,
Holding to Your strength only then I can stand.

As I worship You, Lord, on Your Word, I'll heed,
You are worthy of honor, Your presence I need.

Abundant peace comes to fill moments of time,
As sweet joy flows from Your heartbeat to mine.

Your arms are a stronghold to all who are weak,
It is only You, Lord, hearts and souls must seek.

February 10
ETERNAL FORGIVENESS IS FREE

In Him we have redemption through His blood,
the forgiveness of sins, according to the riches of His grace.
Ephesians 1:7 (NKJV)

Growing closer to You, Lord, it is a wonderful place.
My soul is filled with joy for Your matchless grace.

Your mercy is endless, for eternal forgiveness is free,
I owe all thanks to You and forever I'll honor Thee.

You speak hope into life when I call out Your name.
As long as I live, Your goodness, I'll surely proclaim.

Your peace has victory living deep within my heart,
Nothing compares, and my devotion will never part.

When I am weak Your arms are always open wide,
You take my worries as I'm comforted at Your side.

February 11
LORD, LET MY HEART BE OPEN

---

*Do not be conformed to this world, but be transformed
by the renewal of your mind, that by testing you may
discern what is the will of God, what is good and
acceptable and perfect.*
Romans 12:2 (ESV)

God, I find Your beautiful creation in everything I see,
As Your Spirit whispers quietly Your goodness to me.

Allow me to recognize Your will and always take heed.
Lord, let my heart be open, teach me whatever I need.

Please protect me from desires that do not glorify You,
And purify me for Your purpose in all that I am to do.

Place others in my path allow me to help in every way,
Lord, please speak to me words as we share and pray.

Our lives are changed because You give renewed birth,
All because You came to save and prepare us on earth.

February 12
UNFAILING LOVE

*God showed how much he loved us by sending his one
and only Son into the world so that we might have
eternal life through him.*
1 John 4:9 (NLT)

God, as You direct my journey You are my shining light,
From Heaven, You watch over me by day and by night.

You draw me close while I faithfully seek to follow You,
Help me, Father, keep my eyes upon whatever I'm to do.

In the quietness, Your Holy Spirit gently surrounds me,
My heart is humbled, for Your awesome goodness I see.

Father, I will always praise You for Your unfailing love,
Yet I lack words to express gratefulness to You above.

When I dwell on Your sacrifice for what You've done,
God, I'm so thankful for giving Your One and only Son.

February 13
GUIDING LIGHT

For Your faithful love is before my eyes,
and I live by Your truth.
Psalm 26:3 (HCSB)

Lord, I need Your peace and strength to get through.
Let me walk in faith with Your Spirit as I follow You.

I feel Your presence when in prayer You draw near,
Thank You for mercy as You wipe away every tear.

On this journey, Your Spirit is my true guiding light,
For Your Word says, I am always within Your sight.

When I pray for wisdom, please help me to discern,
As I seek Your will, give me a humble heart to learn.

Lord, let me see through Your eyes Your plan for me,
And to love through Your heart as You hear my plea.

Help me do only Your will, Lord, and lay aside mine.
Please let my life glorify You as I wait in Your time.

February 14
EVERY HEARTBEAT OF LIFE

The LORD is good to those who wait for Him,
To the soul who seeks Him.
Lamentations 3:25 (NKJV)

Lord, You are awesome nothing compares by far,
As the morning sun rises, how precious You are.

I want to follow as You draw nearer each new day,
Lord, as I seek Your will, please show me the way.

You are my peace You help me cope through it all,
As Your strong arms lift me when I can't stand tall.

Trials are weary and some overcome us with pain,
Yet Lord, Your mercy covers us like refreshing rain.

With every heartbeat of life, I want to glorify You,
Bring me close by Your side as we walk through.

February 15
CREATOR OF LIFE

You gave me life and faithful love,
and Your care has guarded my life.
Job 10:12 (HCSB)

You are my God of restoration with power to heal,
As I bow to worship, Your presence is truly real.

You are awesome and faithful to carry me through,
In pain and heartache, God, I totally trust in You.

As I long for answers, please allow my eyes to see,
You're the Creator of life who set this captive free.

Prayers are placed daily into Your heavenly hands,
And I trust You while I wait on Your divine plans.

God, thank You for battles You have faithfully won,
For Your promises give hope found in Your Son.

February 16
Your Hands and Feet

This is what the LORD says-your Redeemer, the Holy One of Israel:
"I am the LORD your God, who teaches you what is good for you
and leads you along the paths you should follow."
Isaiah 48:17 (NLT)

Lord, Your mighty words of truth are firmly spoken,
As You give hope to restored hearts that are broken.

Strengthened while enduring trials I'll trust in You,
I'll forever give You praise as You carry me through.

Thank You, sweet Lord, for kindly watching over me.
My love and devotion will eternally belong to Thee.

Speak to me from Your heart so I don't miss a beat,
Show me ways to be Your hands and guide my feet.

When I try to follow please forgive me when I fail,
My eyes are on You, Lord, I know You will prevail.

February 17
Following Where You Lead

"I have said these things to you, that in me you may have peace.
In the world you will have tribulation. But take heart;
I have overcome the world."
John 16:33 (ESV)

Lord, thank You for Your merciful light shining on me.
As I travel in unseen places, let Your ears hear my plea.

My faith in You, Father, gives true strength to endure,
For in You dwells eternal hope and love that is secure.

In the storms, as I am tested, I will always run to You,
And my devotion I'll give daily for peace You renew.

Your guidance is all I seek, Lord, and I'll forever need,
This journey is for You and following where You lead.

No matter what may come in life, Your Word is true,
As long as I live, Lord, my trust will always be in You.

February 18
TRUSTING IN YOUR PLAN

---

*The LORD is my strength and shield. I trust him
with all my heart. He helps me, and my heart is
filled with joy. I burst out in songs of thanksgiving.*
Psalm 28:7 (NLT)

Lord, to rest in Your presence is all that I need.
I have dreams of Your coming in mighty speed.

As I trust in Your plan, there is no need to fear,
For Your Word says Your Spirit is always here.

Lord, You never fail giving strength and peace,
Your eternal promises I know will never cease.

I lack words to say how much You mean to me,
You are the most precious treasure ever to be.

Lord, in life I will praise You forever and a day.
Help me to honor You with every word, I pray.

February 19
LIFE'S TRIALS

---

*Now hope does not disappoint, because the love of God has been
poured out in our hearts by the Holy Spirit who was given to us.
Romans 5:5 (NKJV)*

Quiet my mind and heart, Lord, draw me close to You,
Coming into Your presence is what my soul longs to do.

Life's trials are purposed to strengthen along the way,
To teach dependence on You in helping us not to stray.

You give Your promise that struggles will someday end.
Lord, I'll praise only You for delivery around the bend.

Your grace changes us while walking in this earthly life,
As Your Spirit speaks hope, when going through strife.

Father, life is planned by Your design and in Your will,
I am unworthy, but thankful You always love me still.

February 20
WHEN MY CUP IS FULL

"These things have I spoken unto you, that my joy might remain in you,
and that your joy might be full."
John 15:11 (KJV)

Lord, when I'm hurt I will always run to You first.
Only You can heal the pain and quench my thirst.

When my cup is full, Lord, I'll need You even more.
And in the days I am broken, You come to restore.

Your loving kindness is with me on the long path.
You are my shield, Lord, from all the earth's wrath.

In times I have failed yet You have helped me see,
Thank You for Your endless grace granted to me.

Lord, my future is unclear, but in You I do believe,
As I fully trust Your Word, joy and peace, I receive.

February 21
HOPE FOR TOMORROW

---

*I consider that our present sufferings are not worth comparing
with the glory that will be revealed in us.*
Romans 8:18 (NIV)

Lord, as You watch through windows of my soul You see,
The difficult pain and hurt which only You have set free.

My broken heart You've mended and held in Your hands.
A life shattered yet renewed by the design of Your plans.

You have protected me as a child, shielding from harms.
For there is joy and peace as I run to my Father's arms.

Lord, You give hope for tomorrow, Your wisdom I seek.
I'll trust through Your Spirit to hear words You speak.

I won't fear the future no matter where paths may go,
My eyes will always be on You, Lord, for I love You so.

February 22
MY HOPE AND STAY

The eternal God is your refuge,
And underneath are the everlasting arms;
Deuteronomy 33:27 (NKJV)

While in Your presence, God, I feel comfort and peace,
As dark clouds bring shadows, I know fear will cease.

Sometimes our life dreams seem to drift farther apart,
Yet You always remind me You will guard my heart.

Your mercy will hold me with everlasting arms of care.
For I'm filled with joy when I come to You in prayer.

Keep my heart soft, Lord, and never to be one of stone.
Lead me to worship You deeper than I've ever known.

I've learned to trust You in whatever comes my way,
Because I'm devoted, Lord, You are my hope and stay.

February 23
WHILE I WAIT FOR YOUR GENTLE VOICE

*"Have I not commanded you? Be strong and of good courage;
do not be afraid, nor be dismayed, for the LORD your God
is with you wherever you go."*
Joshua 1:9 (NJKV)

Lord, I am so grateful let my heart be molded as clay,
Guide me for it is Your voice I need to hear each day.

Thinking of You, Lord, how I love to praise Your name,
Your beautiful promises will forever remain the same.

There's nothing more that I desire but Your embrace,
Thank You, Lord, for Your love and Your divine grace.

I was held in Your hands as You wrote my life story.
My heart is humbled for mercy that flows from glory.

When life seems out of control, You see me through,
It is not for me to understand, but only follow You.

I come, Lord, pouring out my heart on bended knee,
While I wait for Your gentle voice in whispers to me.

February 24
TEARS OF JOY

Rejoice in the Lord always; again I will say, rejoice.
Philippians 4:4 (ESV)

God, Your blessings granted to me I do not deserve.
But I'm thankful it is You, I'll always want to serve.

As I live each day, You are here to take me through,
Deep within my mind, I dwell upon thoughts of You.

I accepted You long ago as You pulled me out of sin,
You healed, saved my soul, and helped to begin again.

You're my heart's treasure, Lord, I will always keep,
You hear as I praise You and see tears of joy I weep.

No matter what comes my way, for You I will stand.
And on the journey I'll follow the path You planned.

February 25
EVERY PAGE OF LIFE

Jesus answered, "I am the way and the truth and the life.
No one comes to the Father except through me."
John 14:6 (NIV)

Lord, You have abundantly blessed through the years.
The chapters are filled with love, laughter, and tears.

You have written every page of life all for Your glory,
You strengthen through trials in everyone's life story.

Trusting You gives peace and through it all, it is well.
You are the only One I seek, in Your goodness I dwell.

Some days the walk is difficult, the steps I cannot see,
Yet as You guide, my faith has always rested in Thee.

My heart is Yours, Lord, I will follow You every day,
Take my hopes and dreams and mold them Your way.

February 26
You Came to Rescue

*You will live in joy and peace. The mountains and hills will
burst into song, and the trees of the field will clap their hands!
Isaiah 55:12 (NLT)*

You are the glorious God of perfection always on time,
No matter the length of the valley or mountains I climb.

Your grace brings happiness more than I've ever known,
No one has loved more for on the Cross You have shown.

Lord, I'm so unworthy, yet You came to rescue my heart,
I will always need You with never a desire to be apart.

Your Word says to go in joy and be led forth with peace.
I will follow You, trusting my trials and pain will cease.

Daily hope is renewed by Your promises from above.
My faith is in You, Lord, and forever You have my love.

February 27
LORD, SOME DAYS I STRUGGLE

*So we must not get tired of doing good, for we will
reap at the proper time if we don't give up.
Galatians 6:9 (HCSB)*

As I pour out my heart, Lord, I know You feel my pain,
Yet Your peace covers me as I whisper Your Holy Name.

You are my Savior and through it all You strengthen me,
Whatever Your plan, I desperately need Your eyes to see.

Lord, some days I struggle to know how or what to pray,
But Your Spirit goes before me, finding the words to say.

Your Word is good and true growing deep within my soul,
Lord, I'm thankful for protection as trials seek to control.

You are steadfast and secure on Your foundation I stand,
I place my faith in You, Lord, walking where You planned.

February 28
KEEPER OF MY HEART

The LORD is your Keeper;
the LORD is your shade on your right hand.
Psalm 121:5 (ESV)

God, Your creation is beyond measure amazing and true.
As stars shine in the moonlight, thoughts dwell on You.

You can quiet the ocean's roar and whisper to the sea,
Yet Lord, Your gentle Spirit faithfully walks beside me.

Your beauty in the night gives sweet peace to my soul,
For You're the keeper of my heart, Lord, I give control.

I'll praise You as I weather through storms and strife,
I have peace, for You are the faithful anchor in my life.

Your Word says You watch over from Heaven above,
I thank You, Lord, for Your sacrifice and endless love.

February 29
ANSWERS WRITTEN IN YOUR PLANS

In the day when I cried out, You answered me,
And made me bold with strength in my soul.
Psalm 138:3 (NKJV)

I long for You, Lord, and envision Your throne,
The mercy You've given, I will claim for my own.

When night fades and sunrise brings a new day,
I sense Your gentle whisper calling me to pray.

I kneel admiring Your beauty in this quiet place.
As I think on Your presence and seek Your face.

While trials and burdens create an anxious heart,
Your love comforts for You care about every part.

I trust my prayers are held secure in Your hands.
And I believe answers are written in Your plans.

You are the strength rooted deep within my soul,
Lord, I leave all at Your feet and in Your control.

March

March 1
WHEN OUR PATH SEEMS LOST

Blessed is everyone who fears the LORD,
who walks in his ways!
Psalm 128:1 (ESV)

There is power in You, Lord, with unfailing grace.
I listen to hear Your voice as I imagine Your face.

My heart is content while resting in who You are,
I look to You, Lord, for You are the greatest by far.

Without You life has only worry and empty hope,
And through all of life's fears, I could never cope.

Every trial has been for my good as I trust in You,
While I walk in Your ways You bring me through.

When our path seems lost we should look above,
As all our answers are found in Your divine love.

March 2
As We Journey Each Day

*Then Jesus spoke to them again: "I am the light of the world.
Anyone who follows Me will never walk in the darkness but will
have the light of life."*
John 8:12 (HCSB)

God, I'm so grateful for Your promises and Your plan.
I know You watch over me with Your faithful hand.

Your strength removes weakness restoring our hope,
I'm truly blessed because You always help me cope.

Lord, my heart overflows with love for You are so dear,
I desire always to please You and Your voice to hear.

The seasons of life bring change as the young grow old,
For our future rests with You, whatever life will hold.

I thank You, God, as we journey each day with peace.
Your gentleness surrounds me as all troubles cease.

When the setting of the sun brings darkness of night,
We will walk in true assurance of Your divine light.

March 3
MY SHINING STAR

Therefore, let us offer through Jesus a continual sacrifice
of praise to God, proclaiming our allegiance to his name.
Hebrews 13:15 (NLT)

Lord, I walk by faith, my love is an offering to You.
I will always worship and honor You in all that I do.

I'm grateful You're here for mountains seem so steep.
As troubled waters of this world grow fiercely deep.

Yet after storms, You paint rainbows in blue skies,
Your blessings are beyond beauty of every sunrise.

There is no end to Your grace or pain You can't cure,
As we cling to You amid trials, we learn to endure.

In silence I think of You and how precious You are,
You give me joy and forever will be my shining star.

March 4
I Will Not Be Afraid

For they all saw Him and were terrified. Immediately He spoke with them and said, "Have courage! It is I. Don't be afraid."
Mark 6:50 (HCSB)

Dear Lord, You know the concern that brings me here.
Yet my soul has peace for Your hands hold every tear.

While I listen for Your whisper of words You speak,
I really need You, Lord, and in Your presence I seek.

If hearts are broken, You always help through it all,
For we are not to worry, Your arms won't let us fall.

In dark valleys You have never left me on my own,
Because of Your Holy Spirit, I will never walk alone.

I will not be afraid whenever trials come my way,
For into Your arms I will run faithfully every day.

March 5
Every Fallen Tear

They that sow in tears shall reap in joy.
Psalm 126:5 (KJV)

Lord, You are comfort to me when the days are gray,
I want to be close by Your side, never losing my way.

When I pray, fear leaves while peace surrounds me,
Your abundant love brings joy and goodness, I see.

Every thought and silent prayer You faithfully hear,
As I remain at Your feet, You catch every fallen tear.

Your everlasting hope provides true strength to rise,
You are the wonderful One who is gentle and wise.

I praise You for Your Word in making Yourself real,
Lord, my heart is Yours, for in Your presence I kneel.

March 6
EVERLASTING HOPE

"The LORD is my portion," says my soul,
"therefore I hope in Him!"
Lamentations 3:24 (NKJV)

I see Your presence in the beauty of this glorious day,
As I wait, Lord, I am listening for what You have to say.

My deep love for You makes devotion grow stronger,
Lord, this is my promise to You not myself any longer.

Troubles come yet I'm assured with You I can weather,
My concerns are removed every time we are together.

You are my Savior, beautiful Lord, and my only King,
With humble praise to Your name, I will joyfully sing.

Lord, we will walk together this journey You planned.
As You give everlasting hope, on Your truth I'll stand.

March 7
OUR LIFE JOURNEY

---

*While we look not at the things which are seen, but at the things
which are not seen: for the things which are seen are temporal;
but the things which are not seen are eternal.*
2 Corinthians 4:18 (KJV)

Lord, You hear my heart as I take each breath of air.
With love and peace, I come to You daily in prayer.

As Your Holy Spirit sees all the difficulty and pain,
Yet You never fail, Lord, to remove the earthly stain.

Our life journey we cannot see but Your eyes can,
For Your Word tells us our eternity is in Your plan.

While waiting on You I'll pour out all my concern,
But wisdom is needed before we can ever learn.

Lord, I rest in Your presence living life Your way,
And whatever comes close to You, I want to stay.

March 8
THROUGH YOUR GRACE

*Grace and peace be multiplied unto you through
the knowledge of God, and of Jesus our Lord,*
2 Peter 1:2 (KJV)

Lord, I seek Your presence at Your altar again.
I'm thankful Your love and mercy have no end.

I commit my life to a love that is deep and true,
My heart is full of grateful praise for only You.

Thank You for the promises You've given to me.
For only in Your presence is where I want to be.

Help me as I walk through the valleys unafraid,
Lord, I know You heard each time I've prayed.

You are strength and shelter as I seek Your will,
In silence I'm reminded, "Just wait and be still."

In lessons I've learned, You've helped me see,
Through Your grace, we can be eternally free.

March 9
HEAVENLY HEIRS

The one who conquers will have this heritage,
and I will be his God and he will be my son.
Revelation 21:7 (ESV)

You are the God of all glory with compassion and love,
You're my great Master watching over me from above.

Let the truth of Your Word grow deep within my heart,
And my faith to be refined throughout, not just in part.

As the storms of trial come Your presence will prevail,
You're the strong anchor, the enemy's lies cannot avail.

No matter what life brings, You are the One who cares,
For we are Your children and one day heavenly heirs.

We are assured of Your strength and where we stand,
Because of Your promise, Lord, our life is all planned.

March 10
The Light of Your Word

*And this is the message which we have heard from him and announce
unto you, that God is light, and in him is no darkness at all.*
1 John 1:5 (ASV)

Lord, You are the One who can set my direction clear.
When I feel as if my path is lost, You are always here.

There is no better place I want to be except with You,
For in the valley, I am grateful You bring me through.

In those moments I am tired I can't find words to say,
It is You, Lord, who speaks whenever I kneel to pray.

It is Your arms that comfort me throughout the years,
And Your goodness makes smiles out of all my tears.

When the storms come with skies of black and gray,
Lord, the light of Your Word casts all darkness away.

March 11
HELP ME GROW DAILY

But whoever lives by the truth comes into the light,
so that it may be seen plainly that what they have done
has been done in the sight of God.
John 3:21 (NIV)

Lord, I long to be with You reading Your Word.
Help me share with others what I have heard.

Please let Your inspiring light flow through me.
So Your beautiful reflection shines for all to see.

I truly want to please You with all I say and do,
Lord, help me grow daily, to learn more of You.

Let me hear Your voice speaking to my heart.
And allow Your goodness to cover every part.

Lord, I thank You for peacefulness in my soul,
For life troubles can no longer take their toll.

March 12
On Your Promises I Stand

For this God is our God for ever and ever;
he will be our guide even unto the end.
Psalm 48:14 (NIV)

God, You came to restore our soul, offering new hope.
You have renewed faith when it was difficult to cope.

You came for brokenness, in trust You see us through.
While walking long journeys, I will always look to You.

You came to grant forgiveness, teaching how to love.
As grace from Your throne, flows gently from above.

You came with endless strength to lift us every hour.
You are Eternal God who holds all might and power.

You came to provide our needs, made by Your hand.
Lord, You came to guide, on Your promises I stand.

March 13
UNCONDITIONAL LOVE

So now faith, hope, and love abide, these three;
but the greatest of these is love.
1 Corinthians 13:13 (ESV)

Lord, weakness is made perfect by strength in You.
When I falter, You lift me up to carry me through.

Your presence is stronger than any trials or strife,
I'll praise You, Lord, for Your victories in my life.

Your words of hope and joy are wonderfully true,
All I will ever need I've found by trusting in You.

I truly want to please You, Lord, in the way I live.
With a humble heart and one that will freely give.

Your unconditional love brings peace to my soul,
As I strive to keep focused on my heavenly goal.

March 14
THE GOD OF GRACE

Now the Lord is the Spirit: and where
the Spirit of the Lord is, there is liberty.
2 Corinthians 3:17 (ASV)

When trials rain on life, Lord, You are always there,
You pour down Your protection for You deeply care.

You're the God of grace, offering freedom from sin,
You ask for our hearts and Your Spirit lives within.

As joy and peace enter, new journeys we can see,
But no place for worries, it is not Your plan to be.

As our strong shield You faithfully go on before us,
You give strength in weakness as we learn to trust.

In our lives the enemy's darkness can't ever hold,
Because of You, Lord, we will stand tall and bold.

March 15
A LOVE THAT IS STRONGER

We love him, because he first loved us.
1 John 4:19 (KJV)

Walking through this valley, Lord, I know You're near,
You have a love that is stronger than any trial or fear.

Help me to be acceptable and pleasing in Your sight.
To leave behind earthly ideas led only by Your light.

Lord, teach me Your faithfulness no matter the cost.
Whatever I go through with You, my life is never lost.

I don't know Your plan or the path You're taking me,
Where ever it is I trust it's where You want me to be.

You've brought me to this place and I know You hear,
You listen to every prayer, catching every single tear.

When pressures of life fade and the end is in sight,
I will bow in praise, Lord, for all things will be right.

March 16
DRAW ME CLOSE, LORD

The LORD is nigh unto all them that call upon him,
to all that call upon him in truth.
Psalm 145:18 (KJV)

Lord, I desperately need You to lead me through.
In this valley, I'll patiently wait to hear from You.

I won't doubt or wonder what You have planned,
Your promises are true, for on Your Word I stand.

Yet in this hard trial I struggle with what to pray,
You see my heart, Lord, help me be strong today.

Draw me close, Lord, I will faithfully praise You,
As You bring me nearer, reveal what I am to do.

You are my guide as I follow You along the way,
Thank You for strength sustaining me each day.

March 17
ETERNITY IS HELD IN YOUR HAND

And pray in the Spirit on all occasions with all kinds of prayers and requests. With this in mind, be alert and always keep on praying for all the Lord's people.
Ephesians 6:18 (NIV)

I worship You, God, I'm so humbled by Your grace.
Thank You for Your presence in this special place.

As I sit in prayer, I think how wonderful You are,
I praise You for the blessings of bringing me so far.

Lord, there's no one who loves as much as You do.
And no one I can confide in the way I do with You.

If the answers are delayed or will never be there,
I believe You haven't forgotten; I know You care.

Your Word says to trust through faith we receive,
Even if there are doubts, we still need to believe.

I pray for those who turn and reject Your plan,
Lord, let them see eternity is held in Your hand.

March 18
REIGN IN ME

I am counting on the LORD; yes, I am counting on him.
I have put my hope in his word.
Psalm 130:5 (NLT)

Reign in me, Lord, the beauty of who You are,
You are the Master of the sun and every star.

I'm so thankful for grace that flows from You,
Because of hope I'm filled each day through.

You deserve all honor, worthy to be praised.
Your name I lift high, Your love I'm amazed.

You are the mighty God of Heaven and earth,
Your strength is far beyond all highest worth.

Reign in me, Lord, joy found in Your name.
For You came to save from sin and shame.

March 19
WAITING THROUGH TESTING

Don't worry about anything, but in everything,
through prayer and petition with thanksgiving,
let your requests be made known to God.
Philippians 4:6 (HCSB)

As I humbly seek in Your presence, Lord, I love You so.
I wonder about the trials today and how I am to grow.

In waiting through testing, Lord, help me see Your plan.
Remind me not to worry as You hold tight to my hand.

I trust in Your faithfulness because I know of Your care,
The end of the valley is coming and soon we'll be there.

Your ears have heard my prayers, for I'm truly blessed.
I lay it all down to You, Lord, and come to You for rest.

While I cling to You for strength You carry me through,
And by faith I will patiently wait for answers from You.

March 20
While in Quiet Times

"In repentance and rest is your salvation,
in quietness and trust is your strength ...
Isaiah 30:15 (NIV)

Lord, I'm strong in weakness because of You.
No other can gently comfort the way You do.

When storms come and wind blows hard rain,
You are with me through fear and all the pain.

As Your Spirit guides, it is always You I seek,
While in quiet times, I wait to hear You speak.

Miracles will come I believe this when I pray,
You are the hope I need as I walk on my way.

Your presence is my refuge I trust and wait,
For I know Your answers are never too late.

March 21
AS WE TRUST IN PRAYER

Even if you should suffer for righteousness' sake,
you will be blessed ...
1 Peter 3:14 (ESV)

With You, Lord, I will never have to walk alone.
You give peace far more than any I have known.

When life crumbles leaving no strength to cope,
We search through brokenness for signs of hope.

The strong winds overtake us during the storm,
As trials come without warning and life is torn.

Lord, You are the strength as we trust in prayer,
You won't abandon us, for You're always there.

As I think of how much You have done for me,
Through all joy and pain, Your blessings I see.

March 22
GRATEFUL FOR GRACE

*And all are justified freely by his grace through
the redemption that came by Christ Jesus.
Romans 3:24 (NIV)*

I trust You, Lord, to guide through this day.
And by Your side is where I want to stay.

My heart bursts with joy in thinking of You,
No one can comfort me in the ways You do.

Life is in Your timing as You have planned,
I seek, Lord, to walk with You hand in hand.

I'm grateful for grace You've always shown,
And for precious moments with You alone.

You are wonderful and I praise You in awe,
I thank you for mercy through every flaw.

March 23
MIRACLES ARE BLESSINGS

Though I walk in the midst of trouble, You preserve my life;
You stretch out Your hand against the wrath of my enemies,
and Your right hand delivers me.
Psalm 138:7 (ESV)

Miracles belong to You, God, in Your perfect time.
We must trust because there is not always a sign.

You can make a heart soft from one that is stone,
And Your Word says You will not leave us alone.

Days are serene while spending them with You,
Yet in the valley You always bring me through.

If waters are rough You faithfully calm the sea,
And when I call Your name, You're here by me.

Miracles are blessings that only You can give,
Through answered prayers in this life, we live.

March 24
ALL ABOUT REDEMPTION

"For God so loved the world, that he gave his only Son,
that whoever believeth on him should not perish,
but have eternal life."
John 3:16 (ESV)

God, You are my strength each day I look to You,
I'm so thankful You are here to see me through.

Always guide my desires to remain in Your will,
Help me in waiting, Lord, teach me to be still.

You have given peace and faith to help me cope,
And I ask favor as I pray for wisdom and hope.

As You look deep in my soul You always know,
How joy fills my heart because I love You so.

The troubles of life really do not matter at all,
It is all about redemption and when You call.

March 25
REFLECTION OF YOU

Let your gentleness be evident to all. The Lord is near.
Philippians 4:5 (NIV)

Lord, Your amazing peace brings tears to my eyes,
As I praise You with joy, my faith begins to rise.

Allow me to hear Your words whenever You speak,
Help me to have a spirit that is caring and meek.

There is no other desire but to glorify Your name,
Even when life changes, You always stay the same.

Let me be a reflection of You, for others to know.
With a life of compassion, Lord, as only You show.

Thank You for mercy, yet I do not deserve You,
Lord, I only want to follow and please in all I do.

March 26
WHEN LIFE IS TESTED

Test me, LORD, and try me, examine my heart and my mind;
Psalm 26:2 (NIV)

Lord, help me understand why plans begin to fall.
Why questions lack answers with no vision at all.

The difficult trials in life are hard to get through,
But faith teaches trust in whatever we have to do.

Lord, heal the hurt that reaches deep to our soul,
Help us let go of fear that readily takes control.

As dreams appear as faint shadows in the sand,
Our hopes are not gone, You have it all planned.

When life is tested, You remind me I'm not alone.
As I look at blessings, You have faithfully shown.

March 27
MY HEAVENLY FATHER

Now unto our God and Father be the glory for ever and ever.
Philippians 4:20 (ASV)

Life is worth living filled with blessings You give,
Close to Your heart, Lord, is where I desire to live.

Your presence fills my soul with Your gentle peace,
As You hear my prayers, all earthly trials cease.

You are my Heavenly Father and praises I'll sing,
Basking in Your goodness, Lord, for You are King.

Abundant strength and hope I find only in You,
I am devoted to You, Lord, nothing else will do.

Thank You for Your mercy and grace given to me.
In quiet times is where I'm drawn closer to Thee.

March 28
BATTLES ARE VICTORIES WON

Thanks be to God,
who gives us the victory through our Lord Jesus Christ.
1 Corinthians 15:57 (NKJV)

Lord, thank You for granting eternal life and peace.
You came to forgive sins, making our troubles cease.

Your light casts out darkness like the morning sun,
And battles are turned into victories You have won.

Your promise gives true hope, setting hearts aglow.
Even in despairing storms when hard winds blow.

Your divine strength is more than enough to sustain,
For Your love comforts through all the earthly pain.

One day You will return as Redeemer and Holy One,
While holding all power as God's One and only Son.

March 29
WHEN TRIALS COME

*And after you have suffered a little while, the God of all grace,
who has called you to his eternal glory in Christ, will himself restore, confirm,
strengthen, and establish you.*
1 Peter 5:10 (ESV)

In this quiet time, Lord, I come asking You to guide,
As I whisper in prayer, I picture Your arms open wide.

I am a life that is changed for Your Spirit lives in me,
I'm thankful for Your grace because I've been set free.

When trials come, we ask why or how long it will last,
But You say not to worry about the future or the past.

Your peace is more than enough to carry me through,
As praise fills my heart, Lord, I will worship only You.

The love and joy that floods my soul will never cease,
For when my world trembles, You give divine peace.

March 30
THE GIFT OF HOPE

The LORD takes pleasure in those who fear Him,
In those who hope in His mercy.
Psalm 147:11 (NKJV)

With each new day, Lord, I long to be alone with You.
Just to express words of thankfulness for all You do.

Your presence refreshes, as walking in warm rain,
You provide gentle peace while mending life's pain.

During days of testing, You remind me I'm not alone.
The waiting is only a matter of time, this I've known.

Lord, You are the gift of hope sent to us from above.
I am very grateful for Your awesome heavenly love.

I want to be alive in You and for Your Spirit to flow,
In honoring only You, Lord, with joy to always show.

My devotion to You will forever be held in my heart.
No one comes before You or can't tear my love apart.

March 31
THE SHELTER FROM TRIALS

For in the day of trouble he will keep me safe in his dwelling;
he will hide me in the shelter of his sacred tent
and set me high upon a rock.
Psalm 27:5 (NIV)

Lord, in the midst of the storm You bring peace,
Your Spirit comforts me, causing worries to cease.

You're the shelter from trials throughout the day,
As Your arms give rest gently soothing cares away.

Lord, as You quietly whispered my name years ago,
You had a plan before I could ever begin to know.

In You I found a love that is so wonderful and true,
Lord, nothing in my life could ever compare to You.

While I rejoice for the bountiful mercy given to me,
I will praise You, my Lord, for Your blessings I see.

April

April 1
ETERNAL HOPE

For Christ also suffered once for sins, the righteous for the
unrighteous, that he might bring us to God, being put to death
in the flesh but made alive in the spirit.
1 Peter 3:18 (ESV)

Lord, I am sorry how You suffered and died,
So many wouldn't listen because of the pride.

Each step You took carrying the heavy Cross,
Yet You knew it would be to our gain, not loss.

Oh, how sad Your heart truly must have been,
As they plotted against You, driven by the sin.

You freely gave as blood fell on cold ground,
Yet You rose again with eternal hope found.

I'm happy the enemy cannot separate us now,
For my heart is committed and to You I bow.

Lord, I thank You for giving Your grace to me.
For I was blind, but now praise God, I can see.

April 2
In My Quiet Place

"But when you pray, go into your private room, shut your
door, and pray to your Father who is in secret.
And your Father who sees in secret will reward you."
Matthew 6:6 (HCSB)

In my quiet place, Lord, I come to praise only Thee,
For all Your many blessings, oh, how You amaze me.

Life is sometimes an unclear path on a broken road,
With hearts burdened by pain bearing a heavy load.

As endless nights are filled with many a fallen tear,
Lord, I believe amid every trial You are always here.

All my prayers are faithfully cradled in Your hands.
And all the answers are given by Your divine plans.

There is no other to trust, Your promises are true,
In my quiet place, Lord, my faith rests in only You.

April 3
GOOD MORNING, LORD

Glory in his holy name;
Let the hearts of those who seek the Lord rejoice!
1 Chronicles 16:10 (NIV)

Good morning, Lord, Your name warms my heart.
I want to say; I love You before my day will start.

I thank You for Your goodness and constant care,
And I ask forgiveness when I do things in error.

You're the solid Rock giving me strength to stand.
I am content for You hold my heart in Your hand.

You are a treasure with a value I cannot replace.
Joy fills my soul for someday I'll see Your face.

In this quiet daybreak, You have drawn me near.
Just a gentle whisper, Lord, is all I need to hear.

Your unfailing peace and comfort I will proclaim,
As I praise with joy, Lord, glorifying Your name.

April 4
WITHIN YOUR PRESENCE

*The righteous person may have many troubles,
but the LORD delivers him from them all;
Psalm 34:19 (NIV)*

Lord, life is wonderful when I'm alone with You.
All I ask is Your Holy Spirit to guide me through.

Your arms of protection surround me every hour,
I'm grateful for Your goodness and divine power.

It is amazing how earthly worries seem to cease,
For within Your presence, there is joy and peace.

Lord, I'm thankful through brokenness You heal,
For Your whispers are soft yet strong and real.

I love our quiet times when it's just You and me,
Because where You are is where I desire to be.

April 5
DIVINE PROMISE

Jesus said unto her, "I am the resurrection, and the life: he that believeth in me, though he were dead, yet shall he live." John 11:25 (KJV)

God, You are so righteous and holy; I praise You.
Your Word is real, through grace we become new.

I am in awe of the beauty Your hands have made,
And I'm humbled to know my sins You have paid.

Salvation is free with divine promise given to all,
Your Spirit guides us, helping not to waver or fall.

Peace and happiness flows out to those who trust,
For keeping our faith in You, Lord, in life we must.

Your everlasting love is more than enough for me,
Please bless with wisdom, opening my eyes to see.

Teach me more about You as I follow Your ways.
Every moment I will seek You for all of my days.

April 6
When the Journey Is Unseen

"For I know the plans I have for you," declares the LORD,
"plans to prosper you and not for harm you,
plans to give you hope and a future."
Jeremiah 29:11 (NIV)

The very thought of You, God, brings joy when I pray,
As darkness turns to light in Your presence, I'll stay.

My faith becomes strong when I think of Your love,
And I believe You are watching from Heaven above.

With each breath I praise You for grace given to me,
For in the valleys, many times, my eyes failed to see.

No power in this world can ever steal my love away,
Because I trust You, God, my strength will not sway.

You gave Your promises and on Your Word I'll lean.
Even in troubled waters when the journey is unseen.

April 7
In Life's Changing Seasons

For you know that the testing of your faith produces steadfastness.
James 1:3 (ESV)

Lord, as I enter each day with You by my side,
No matter the path, You'll always be my guide.

Your trials are teaching how to grow in grace.
Thank You for strength in this time and place.

In life's changing seasons Your Word is secure,
With steadfast promises, always true and sure.

You're the Savior of my soul and I adore You,
I'm so thankful, God, for carrying me through.

The peace that's given by Your Spirit each day,
Brings forth humble praise as I come to pray.

April 8

IN THE TRIALS

In God, whose word I praise, in God I trust; I will not fear.
What can man do to me?
Psalm 56:4 (HCSB)

Lord, You see the raging storms within my soul,
Yet I will never fear, for You have total control.

Each moment of change my faith remains in You,
There's no doubt You are here to see me through.

You go before me, Lord, on Your Word I'll stand.
For in Your promise, there's power in Your hand.

You come swiftly into battle taking charge of me,
The enemy sees Your presence, and he has to flee.

In the trials, I'm covered by Your peace and love,
With a humble heart, I give praise to You above.

April 9
MASTERPIECES OF LOVE

O Lord, what a variety of things you have made!
In wisdom you have made them all. The earth is full of your creatures.
Psalm 104:24 (NLT)

Lord, Your miracles are blessings You freely give,
It is Your presence in life we have reason to live.

Your glorious creations are masterpieces of love,
You divinely provide as gifts from Heaven above.

As the sun sets, Your radiance shines from on high,
There's vast beauty in the glorious watercolor sky.

Flowers of brilliance opening up to see their face,
As petals dance in the wind with so much grace.

The oceans and beaches boast delicate white sand,
Pictures You paint with one brush of Your hand.

Abundance You have provided because You care,
I will faithfully praise You, Lord, daily in prayer.

April 10
GLORY AND HONOR

LORD, you are my God; I will exalt you and praise your name,
for in perfect faithfulness you have done wonderful things,
things planned long ago.
Isaiah 25:1 (NIV)

Lord, Your beauty is a blessing within each day.
Yet as sunlight fades, Your love never goes away.

There is mercy in Your awesome sweet name,
Your faithfulness is true, I will forever proclaim.

Your ways are never changing, I'll shout for joy.
You make new what the enemy tries to destroy.

I'll seek Your guidance as I travel life through.
And I'll need Your peace, Lord, only You can do.

Forever I will be grateful for all You have done,
You are Savior of all because You are God's Son.

Thankfulness fills my heart, Lord, I humbly owe,
To You glory and honor, I pray my life will show.

April 11
ONE TRUE VINE

---

*"I am the vine; you are the branches. He who abides
in Me, and I in him, bears much fruit;
for without Me you can do nothing."*
John 15:5 (NKJV)

Lord, as I search for guidance of what I'm to do,
I close my eyes to dwell on the nearness of You.

Please speak to my soul as I come quietly to pray,
Your arms provide comfort where I need to stay.

Your promise brings hope when strength is weak,
In Your presence I feel loved, for it is You I seek.

I trust Your ways, Lord, much better than mine,
As I give praise for You are the, "One True Vine."

Thank You, Lord, for providing all I need to live.
As I kneel before You unworthy of all You give.

April 12

LIGHT IN THE WORLD

*"I am come a light into the world, that whosoever believeth
on me should not abide in darkness."*
John 12:46 (KJV)

Lord, I worship You with all my heart and soul,
My worries fade when I give You total control.

You're the light in the world through You I see,
You strengthen the weak and peace sets us free.

I pray for changed lives and hearts to be healed,
You're the only hope, provider and strong shield.

Nothing, Lord, is impossible in this life for You,
Your Word gives directions to guide us through.

Lord, help me never question Your reasons why,
But in every moment lift my eyes to You on high.

Teach me how to reflect Your beauty from above.
And forever share the depth of Your divine love.

April 13
GRACE MAKES ALL NEW

So then let us follow after things which make for peace,
and things whereby we may edify one another.
Romans 14:19 (ASV)

As the rain falls, Lord, it reminds me of tears,
When You gave up life to remove all our fears.

With gentleness You cover all heartfelt sorrow,
You provide peace and rest for every tomorrow.

Your promise replaces any battles we may face.
As we give all to You, we release what we chase.

When the enemy plants old lies into our mind,
Your grace makes all new as You have designed.

You turn bitterness, despair and hearts of stone,
Into love that shares more joy than ever known.

April 14
DWELL IN THANKFULNESS

*Give thanks in all circumstances; for this
is the will of God in Christ Jesus for you.
I Thessalonians 5:18 (ESV)*

There is joy in You, Lord, through sunshine and rain,
You prepare my path as I walk in laughter and pain.

Your name is valued, highest of any treasure in life,
Our mighty defender throughout all earthly strife.

Victories will come in Your time to humble prayer,
So many blessings You give with Your loving care.

It is to You I look for true guidance day after day,
For You are the One who helps me along the way.

I will dwell in thankfulness as long as I shall live,
To honor You, Lord, because of all You freely give.

April 15
THROUGH YOUR EYES

For the LORD your God is the One who goes with you to
fight for you against your enemies to give you victory.
Deuteronomy 20:4 (HCSB)

Guide my steps, Lord, lead with Your loving hand,
There is peace in Your presence, by You I'll stand.

You fought my battles with Your power You won,
As I reflect on Your goodness in all You've done.

Through Your eyes, I see trials in a different light.
For I am no longer in darkness now I have sight.

Brokenness is left behind as I seek You each day,
While hurt is healed and struggles washed away.

Your divine love and grace, Lord, makes life new,
I am so thankful great blessings come from You.

April 16

TRAVELING THE UNSEEN PATH

As for God, his way is perfect; the word of the LORD is tried:
he is a buckler to all them that trust in him.
2 Samuel 22:31 (KJV)

Lord, I'm so thankful I can come to You in prayer.
Because without You life would be hard to bear.

The cry of my heart is always staying close to You,
You are joy to my soul as I live each day through.

Your Spirit comforts, allowing peace to overflow,
And as trust deepens, the more devoted I grow.

In traveling the unseen path You faithfully guide,
All I have needed You have not failed to provide.

As I see all You've created by Your loving hands,
I take refuge every day my life is in Your plans.

April 17
YOU ALWAYS MAKE A WAY

Blessed are You, O LORD! Teach me Your statutes!
Psalm 119:12 (NKJV)

Lord, let me be a beacon reflecting Your love.
Give strength as You watch over from above.

Please direct my footsteps guiding where I go,
Whether high on a mountain or in valleys low.

Walking with You daily is my journey for life,
In You there is hope, no heartaches and strife.

The trials are hard yet in Your time disappear,
For heaviness is gone when You draw me near.

Lord, as I pray in trust, through another day,
I am thankful for how You always make a way.

April 18
AS I WALK BY FAITH

Now faith is the substance of things hoped for,
the evidence of things not seen.
Hebrews 11:1 (KJV)

Lord, You've led to a crossroad where am I to go?
I wait, praying for direction if only I could know.

Thank You for Your Holy Spirit I'm truly blessed,
While I lay trials at Your feet, I receive Your rest.

It's difficult understanding if the path isn't clear,
Yet I trust Your Word, and I know You are here.

My soul has sweet peace You have placed within,
For You came to save us from all shame and sin.

I'll praise You for the love You've shown to me,
Lord, I only want to honor You in all I am to be.

As I walk by faith, I'll trust You to show the way,
For You see what lies ahead through every day.

April 19
The Only Path There Is

Your Word is a lamp to guide my feet and a light to my path.
Psalm 119:105 (NLT)

God, You are wonderful every minute of each day.
The unseen plans are exciting as I walk Your way.

Let Your light shine through wherever I shall go,
To honor You is the only path there is to know.

You have heard my cry many times I've been sad,
Yet for blessings You give, I'm humbled and glad.

In weakness, when strength seems to fall away,
Your Spirit faithfully guides me back when I pray.

Lord, thank You for peace You faithfully bestow.
Your presence brings joy, I always want to show.

April 20
As Roots Grow Deep

But grow in grace, and in the knowledge of our Lord and Savior Jesus Christ. To him be glory both now and forever.
2 Peter 3:18 (KJV)

Above soft clouds I look as far as I can see,
Lord, I know You watch faithfully over me.

I'm blessed walking with You day after day,
Thank You, Lord, for guiding along the way.

While Your Spirit speaks in this quiet place,
I close my eyes to imagine Your loving face.

As roots grow deep to the depth of Your love,
I surrender my life to Your arms from above.

Let my words be pure as praise fills my heart,
With glory to You, Lord, who owns every part.

The moment I found You, my life became new.
And the more I understood, my love only grew.

April 21
In Life Storms

---

*"So be strong and courageous! Do not be afraid and do not panic
before them. For the LORD your God will personally go ahead
of you. He will neither fail you nor abandon you."*
Deuteronomy 31:6 (NLT)

Lord, there's been days I have run to You to hide.
And in those valleys You have never left my side.

I'll trust in Your plan for You know what is best,
While in Your presence, I am completely at rest.

In life storms You cover me with Your firm hands,
And as winds grow fierce, Your Word still stands.

I'm truly blessed and humbly want You to know,
As I dwell on Your mercies, the praises overflow.

Lord, there's no one in life I need more than You,
For Your abundant peace is so precious and true.

April 22
WHEREVER YOU LEAD

Let the wise hear and increase in learning,
and the one who understands obtain guidance.
Proverbs 1:5 (ESV)

Lord, You have brought me through unknown ways.
In deserts traveled while You have guided my days.

There is a deep joy in the midst of all life's sorrow,
Because Your Spirit is with me in every tomorrow.

Lord, many times I've asked for comfort and peace.
And You gave mercy by telling the trials to cease.

I'm humbled for each moment together we share,
In those precious times, I feel how much You care.

Lord, let me learn in following wherever You lead.
My heart is grateful You give far more than I need.

April 23
THE GRAND DESIGNER

God made the earth by His power; He established the world
by His wisdom and by His understanding
and skill stretched out the heavens.
Jeremiah 10:12 (AMPC)

Lord, nothing else compares to Your beauty or worth.
You are the grand designer of all Heaven and earth,

Even in the deepest valleys and we can't see the way,
As we trust You, Lord, we grow stronger day by day.

Your Word gives hope as Your power removes fears,
Soon there will be no more worries, no more tears.

Lord, life is all about You, please guide by Your hand.
Never to be my will but to live as You have planned.

You are the One of divine peace and only One I need,
Lord, I look for the day You'll return in mighty speed.

April 24
Grant Me a Servant's Heart

Therefore, my dear brothers and sisters, stand firm. Let nothing
move you. Always give yourselves fully to the work of the Lord,
because you know that your labor in the Lord is not in vain.
1 Corinthians 15:58 (NIV)

Lord, to kneel as I wait for You is a humbled pleasure.
For Your voice, as I seek, is my most valued treasure.

Teach me to be mindful of what You want me to learn,
And Lord, forgive me for worry over earthly concern.

Lord, please grant Your wisdom, for in You I'll rest.
And if fears arise, please remind me, You know best.

In the weakest moments let me always lean on You,
Because in my heart I know You'll take me through.

Grant me a servant's heart to reflect Your true love,
To know Your will, Lord, as I stay close to You above.

April 25
BLESSINGS FOR ANOTHER SEASON

For the vision is yet for the appointed time; it testifies about the end and will not lie. Though it delays, wait for it, since it will certainly come and not be late.
Habakkuk 2:3 (HCSB)

Lord, in the quiet moments I come to seek Your will,
I'm waiting, yet I understand if You desire to be still.

If questions have no answers, it is for Your reason,
Perhaps for testing or blessings for another season.

My heart is devoted, Lord, and trusts in You alone.
I thank You for peace that flows from Your throne.

When our path is unknown, You show us the way,
You are faithful, I will praise You every time I pray.

Even with delays in Your appointed time and place,
Lord, I will remain thankful for Your hand of grace.

April 26

WALKING THIS JOURNEY

Even though I walk through the darkest valley,
I will fear no evil, for you are with me;
Psalm 23:4 (NIV)

Day after day passes, Lord, while I wait on You,
As strong winds blow, yet You bring me through.

Some battles may be lost but they do not matter,
Because all that's important won't ever shatter.

Lord, through my darkest times You never leave,
For You know my heart and how much I believe.

The joy and peace is beyond anything to compare,
Nothing equals Your presence and amazing care.

Walking this journey may often be one of mystery,
But at the end of time we have a heavenly victory.

April 27
THROUGH EVERY BATTLE

In all these things we are more than conquerors
through him that loved us.
Romans 8:37 (KJV)

Lord, my heart is filled with praise I honor You,
You are the only One guiding me safely through.

Every moment I know You see my thirsty heart,
Because Lord, I have been Yours from the start.

The peace overflows as I dwell on Your name,
I'm humbled and glad my life is Yours to reign.

Through every battle, You're mighty and strong,
With You beside me, I have a purpose and song.

We become weathered whenever the winds blow,
Yet I look to You, Lord, my joy will forever flow.

April 28
HUMBLE TEARS

Therefore, as God's chosen people, holy and dearly loved,
clothe yourselves with compassion, kindness, humility,
gentleness and patience.
Colossians 3:12 (NIV)

God of grace and peace Your presence is divine,
Lord, I give honor as I kneel, for Your joy is mine.

Serenity arrives each morning with every sunrise,
I think of You as I look to the magnificent skies.

For Your loving kindness I'll thank You every day,
And all life's trials I will give You as I bow to pray.

You are strength, I won't be moved as winds blow,
I will stand firm in You as my praises sincerely flow.

Allow my worship to be a sweet song in Your ears.
While Your gentle hands hold all my humble tears.

You're worth more than any treasure life will give,
Lord, let my words magnify You each moment I live.

April 29
As I Bow to Praise

My lips will glorify you because your faithful love is better than life.
Psalm 63:3 (CSB)

Lord, I imagine You watching down from glory,
While I give You humble praise for my life story.

Each time I seek Your presence to sit at Your feet,
You turn the painful trials into memories sweet.

I have strength and peace that only You can give,
Because serving You, Lord, I have purpose to live.

When dark clouds come to overshadow my days,
I gladly call upon Your name as I bow to praise.

Thank You for a love that is awesome and true.
For I know all good things come only from You.

Lord, to You nothing compares or values more.
As I walk with You, I trust whatever is in store.

April 30
AS WE WALK THROUGH VALLEYS

*And we know that all things work together for good
to them that love God, to them who are the called
according to his purpose.*
Romans 8:28 (KJV)

Lord, in You I put my faith, for Your love is true.
Your blessings flow from Heaven fresh and new.

When it's difficult to move on and hard to let go,
I cry out, Lord, seeking for the way I don't know.

In times of trial You strengthen and refine hope,
  As we walk through valleys, You help us cope.

I'll cling to You, Lord, when my struggles begin,
  And stay by Your side because You always win.

Life is safe in Your hands for You hold my fate,
Nothing for You is impossible and never too late.

May

May 1
HOPE FOR TODAY AND EVERY TOMORROW

In the same way, wisdom is sweet to your soul.
If you find it, you will have a bright future and
your hopes will not be cut short.
Proverbs 24:14 (NLT)

Lord, Your strength comes amid our pain and sorrow,
As Your hand gives hope today and every tomorrow.

You are the everlasting peace and my priceless friend.
Heartaches vanish as fears melt and scars You mend.

Lord, You're faithful in valleys and sovereign over us,
For what the enemy means as evil, You turn into trust.

Compassion and kindness are gifts flowing from You,
Let those searching find grace to bring them through.

Lord, give them the desire to draw closer to Your side.
To know Your love is deeper than all the oceans wide.

May 2
PRECIOUS MOMENTS

"But seek ye first the kingdom of God, and his righteousness;
and all these things shall be added unto you."
Matthew 6:33 (KJV)

Throughout eternity, Lord, You are totally divine,
As You guide us, Your presence will always shine.

I see blessings revealed in Your star filled skies,
While joy fills my heart, beauty delights my eyes.

When darkness fades, in comes a brand new day,
And goodness and mercy leads us along the way.

While I walk this journey You've intended for me,
I search Your will, that's how life is planned to be.

Lord, every day I pray and You are always there,
In those precious moments, that You and I share.

You're the Savior of my soul as love runs so deep,
In my heart Your name, Lord, I will forever keep.

May 3
ABUNDANT GRACE

"Seek the LORD while he may be found;
call on him while he is near."
Isaiah 55:6 (NIV)

Lord, deeper in love with You I grow day after day.
Draw me nearer to Your side where I want to stay.

You stir within my soul a longing for more of you,
Only You satisfy my needs the perfect way You do.

I like to imagine the forgiving smile on Your face.
With Your arms surrounding in abundant grace.

Your peace comforts more than I've ever known.
As joy gently flows from Your heavenly throne.

To dwell in Your presence is everything to me,
Lord, there is no other place that I desire to be.

May 4
THE SECURE TOWER

*You will keep him in perfect peace, Whose mind is stayed
on You, Because he trusts in You.*
Isaiah 26:3 (NKJV)

There was a rainbow tonight You sent for all to see,
It is a sign of Your promise, Lord, as it reminded me.

Spectacular beauty You provide in this world we live,
Yet many take for granted all the blessings You give.

In quietness I'll wait while spending time with You,
As I'm thankful for each day You bring me through.

You are the One to trust and only One we will need.
For in Your presence I long and Your Word I heed.

You are healer of hearts, Your hands hold them all,
You are the secure tower who helps us stand tall.

May 5
MY ETERNAL ROCK

He is the Rock, his work is perfect: for all his ways are judgment:
A God of truth and without iniquity, just and right is he.
Deuteronomy 32:4 (KJV)

Lord, my soul is renewed each time I come to You,
Your arms of restoration always bring me through.

You are my eternal Rock and precious safe place,
You give hope as trials arise and fear You erase.

Nothing comes against me that shall ever stand,
You hold my life and heart firmly in Your hand.

Assurance You give every moment I'm with You,
I'll honor You, Lord, for Your promises are true.

Your peace is provided by faithfully being here,
As Your comforting hands wipe away every tear.

I trust in You, Lord, forgive me in the times I fail,
I thank You for Your Word, it will always prevail.

May 6
ASSURANCE IN THE DARKEST HOUR

For Thou hast been my shelter for me,
And a strong tower from the enemy.
Psalm 61:3 (KJV)

Lord, You're the Master over my soul protecting me.
Through storms, Your divine light gives sight to see.

Your presence strengthens my spirit, removing fear,
With You I am never alone, I'm glad You are here.

As Your peace comforts by Your side I want to stay,
I trust how You watch over me by night and day.

Your grace allows us to rise above guilt and shame.
You're the healer of all for joy rests in Your name.

Thank you for assurance even in the darkest hour,
I am always secure for You, Lord, hold all power.

May 7
GRACE FILLED STRENGTH

"Fear not, for I am with you; be not dismayed, for I am your God;
I will strengthen you, I will help you, I will uphold you
with my righteous right hand."
Isaiah 41:10 (ESV)

Lord, peace comforts me as I come to You in prayer.
My needs You've provided with each breath of air.

Resting in silence my thoughts are filled with You,
As I whisper my praise, I'm thankful for all You do.

In Your grace filled strength is how I desire to live,
I need You, Lord, far more than anything I can give.

You've gently mended this broken heart of mine,
Lord, there is no other who is so loving and kind.

I will always praise You every day that passes by,
You hear my prayers and You know when I cry.

As I come to You in prayer, I give my trials to You.
Lord, it's in Your timing, all things are made new.

May 8
THE ARTIST

"You are worthy, O Lord,
To receive glory and honor and power; For You created
all things, And by Your will they exist and were created."
Revelation 4:11 (NKJV)

Thank You God, for beauty in this world we live,
And for goodness and mercies You faithfully give.

While I gaze up to the boundless clouds on high,
You've painted a glorious rainbow filling the sky.

I see the soft rays of light filtering down through,
As I pretend it's coming directly to me from You.

I envision an image of an eagle flying with ease,
You're the artist, God, who truly paints to please.

There is spectacular color in the rising of the sun,
As Your creation reveals miracles, You have done.

In my thoughts I claim any vision I dream to see,
I imagine how beautiful Heaven will someday be.

Life is filled with blessings flowing from above,
Our journey is designed with Your perfect love.

May 9
ENDLESS GRACE

Know therefore that the LORD your God is God,
the faithful God who keeps covenant and steadfast
love with those who love him and keep his commandments.
Deuteronomy 7:9 (RSV)

Lord, in stillness my thoughts are filled with You,
I'm thankful in trials You always see me through.

Your faithfulness prevails each time I'm in need,
I'll always yield my heart in asking You to lead.

You came to comfort our every worry and fear,
And we are strengthened because You are near.

Your presence gives peace with steadfast hope,
I've seen You turn bad into good so I can cope.

In the quiet, Lord, I know You hear my prayer,
And in storms You shelter me because You care.

Oh, Lord, I am grateful for Your endless grace.
Sunrise to sunset, I will forever seek Your face.

May 10
GRACE WILL ALWAYS FLOW

---

*And the grace of our Lord was exceeding abundant
with faith and love which is in Christ Jesus.
1 Timothy 1:14 (KJV)*

God, speak to me as I wait in the quiet for You today.
I long for Your whisper as I listen for what You say.

As raindrops fall in Your abundant beauty I see You,
With winter gone and new birth is peeking through.

When hours pass by and the sun slowly drifts down,
Yet another day comes as the sunrise wears a crown.

The river wanders for miles the journey You know,
It is in Your plan where free grace will always flow.

I pray for words to tell of Your love filling my heart,
For I know God, from You, I never want to be apart.

May 11
LORD, STILL MY MIND

---

*Jesus replied, "But even more blessed are all who hear
the word of God and put it into practice."*
Luke 11:28 (NLT)

Lord, please help me listen to Your voice every day.
Lead me in following Your will while I humbly pray.

Instill in me grace to be forgiving, gentle and meek,
Help me know Your thoughts whenever You speak.

Lord, teach me to submit to what You have in store.
To hear Your heartbeat, there's nothing I want more.

In trials, Lord, still my mind, as I focus only on You,
Help me know the journey for whatever I am to do.

Lord, please quiet my spirit as I humbly praise You.
Thank You for Your presence each moment through.

May 12

REDEEMING BLOOD

But if we walk in the light as He is in the light, we have
fellowship with one another, and the blood of Jesus Christ
His Son cleanses us from all sin.
1 John 1:7 (NKJV)

Lord, I need Your strength, for today I am weak,
I can't see the future, but it is You I always seek.

I am only human created by Your loving hand,
Lord, when You teach, help me to understand.

I don't deserve the blessings, Lord, none at all.
I try not to fail You, but sometimes I still fall.

Lord, I pray to stay close always by Your side.
To be pure in Your sight with nothing to hide.

I am a sinner saved by Your redeeming blood,
As divine grace flowed like a cleansing flood.

May 13
GOD OF MIRACLES

The LORD is my strength and my song;
He has become my salvation.
This is my God, and I will praise Him,
my father's God, and I will exalt Him.
Exodus 15:2 (HCSB)

Lord, Your Word is good, Your Spirit is sweet,
I lay earthly trials and tribulations at Your feet.

You give signs of hope in whatever I go through,
And in Your presence, I'll wait to hear from You.

Even though undeserving of Your love and care,
I come to You in assurance You are always there.

I ask for Your divine will in every request I pray,
As I lift You higher through every night and day.

Nothing is impossible, with You here by my side,
You are the God of Miracles, You always provide.

May 14
STRENGTH FOR TOMORROW

The name of the Lord is a strong tower.
The man who does what is right runs into it and is safe.
Proverbs 18:10 (NLV)

In childlike faith I come to You, my precious Lord,
My soul has been woven with Yours in one accord.

You give new strength for tomorrow; I need it so.
I am assured Your goodness will abundantly flow.

Your light defeats darkness, giving glory to You,
As my faith grows deeper, You bring me through.

My spirit is humble for many answered prayers,
I know You are with me and the One who cares.

I long to be closer, in Your presence I will stay.
As I live striving to honor You every single day.

May 15
MOLD ME, LORD

*For it is all for your sake, so that as grace extends
to more and more people it may increase thanksgiving,
to the glory of God.*
2 Corinthians 4:15 (ESV)

Lord, I honor You because You always care.
No matter what I need, You're always there.

Please help me be open in sharing Your Word,
To tell those around me who have never heard.

Lord, I ask You to mold me into who I'm to be,
Let Your Holy Spirit freely shine through me.

Thank You for guidance, I want to serve You,
Let my life be one of giving in everything I do.

Lord, I come to You in prayer, I humbly bow.
I leave all in Your hands, whatever You allow.

May 16
WASHED IN HUMBLE PRAYER

Humble yourselves in the sight of the Lord,
and he shall lift you up.
James 4:10 (KJV)

Lord, let my words be washed in humble prayer.
As I enter my special place, I know You are there.

You are bigger than any treasure we may possess.
Thank You for Your faithfulness, You kindly bless.

You sometimes allow our hopeful dreams to fail,
So that Your divine purpose will always prevail.

Help me live within Your will, Your desired plan,
Because the design was Yours before life began.

Lord, whatever comes my eyes will look to You,
For in the valley, Your Word carries me through.

Thank You for Your truth and presence in my life.
As trials overwhelm, Your mercy comforts strife.

May 17

WHATEVER COMES WE CAN WEATHER

For everyone born of God overcomes the world. This is the
victory that has overcome the world, even our faith.
1 John 5:4 (NIV)

Lord, my assurance comes from the promises of You.
For in weakness, I'm strong as You carry me through.

The failures are never final in Your everlasting eyes,
With every end, there is always a beautiful sunrise.

Your presence gives hope and in You I'm fully alive,
As we walk through the raging storm, I will survive.

You restored joy while I learned to trust and pray,
As I lay all my trials at Your feet every single day.

Lord, You are the bond that holds my life together.
With You whatever comes, I know we can weather.

May 18

IF ONLY MY HEART COULD SPEAK

*And whatever you do in word or deed, do all in
the name of the Lord Jesus, giving thanks to God
the Father through Him.*
Colossians 3:17 (NKJV)

Lord, I need to be alone with You again today.
I just want to hear what it is You have to say.

In quiet moments I feel joy thinking about You,
For it is in Your presence I can make it through.

I think of Your sunshine and the refreshing rain.
And how You send blessings even through pain.

Your peace gently casts out all the earthly fears,
For Your hand moves softly, wiping away tears.

Your strength holds me up when dreams shatter,
It's Your plan, Lord, that will ever really matter.

If only my heart could speak, what would it say?
Dear Lord, You already know my thoughts today.

May 19
REFUGE FROM WORLDLY FEARS

Trust in him at all times, pour out your heart before him.
God is our refuge.
Psalm 62:8 (CSB)

Lord, as You guide with Your Spirit's light,
Let these words be acceptable in Your sight.

You see my heart and every thought of You,
I'm grateful and assured Your Word is true.

Growing closer makes my soul want to sing,
For it is hope and peace only You can bring.

You are my refuge from the worldly fears,
You carried me away from trials and tears.

I treasure moments pouring out my heart,
I know You listen, caring about every part.

I'll trust because You are my strong shield,
And to You, Lord, everything in life I yield.

May 20
A Heart That Is Broken

*To this you were called, because Christ suffered for you,
leaving you an example, that you should follow in his steps.
1 Peter 2:21 (NIV)*

Lord, help me to live with a heart that is broken.
Let it be filled with deeds of love softly spoken.

Let it never hesitate to give freely when in need,
Yet bold enough with Your words to plant a seed.

Let it be deeply touched by those hurt and crying,
And gently witness to the one who may be dying.

Let it be encouragement to those weak and frail,
Please allow me to help them and to never fail.

Let it humbly seek Your will, trusting as a child.
And to be faithful in ways, to be meek and mild.

Lord, please mold my heart to be honest and true.
To completely surrender and to honor only You.

May 21
A BEACON OF LIGHT

You will seek me and find me,
when you seek me with all your heart.
Jeremiah 29:13 (ESV)

Take me away, Lord, to spend time with You.
I lay my heart at Your feet only You can renew.

I see You in the beauty by the sandy seashore,
You are the Master of life and the One I adore.

To hear Your voice within me is all I want to do,
There is peace every day that I share with You.

Lord, keep me close to You, never letting me go.
And fill me with joy to allow Your love to flow.

Help me be a beacon of light standing for You,
So others see Your strength every day through.

May 22
DO ANGELS WEEP IN HEAVEN?

*And do not make God's Holy Spirit sad; for the Spirit
is God's mark of ownership on you, a guarantee
that the Day will come when God will set you free.*
Ephesians 4:30 (GNT)

Lord, I think of Your tender heart and if You cry,
In the times You are neglected as the years go by.

Do angels weep in Heaven if they see You are sad?
Yet how they must rejoice when Your heart is glad.

Are You grieved when we don't love one another?
And why do we hurt our neighbor or our brother?

We have many battles that try to weigh us down,
When the chains somehow keep us earthly bound.

I will praise as I come into Your presence to pray,
To give honor and glory humbly every single day.

The trials are tough yet our sins You will redeem,
Lord, Your hands hold all hope and every dream.

May 23
A WORSHIP SONG

So I will give thanks to You among the nations, O Lord.
I will sing praises to Your name.
2 Samuel 22:50 (NLV)

As I walk in the garden on this lovely sunlit day,
I thank You, Lord, for such beauty along my way.

I dwell on Your wonderful Word, good and true.
And how You are always faithful in all You do.

So many times I've failed, yet You are still here,
You reached out Your hand, removing my fear.

In valleys I've been lifted by Your strong arms,
Through my trials, You kept me from all harms.

Lord, I'm so grateful I'll praise You all day long.
For Your joy has truly given me a worship song.

May 24
LEAD ME IN YOUR WAYS

---

*Then said Jesus unto his disciples, "If any man would
come after me, let him deny himself, and take up
his cross, and follow me."
Matthew 16:24 (ASV)*

I will praise You God for how great You are,
For all earth's beauty and every bright star.

To draw closer there is nothing I want more,
Lead me in Your ways to whatever is in store.

I'm not to worry for I know it is not of You,
I just need Your strength in walking through.

You are faithful to hear every cry and prayer,
As You give Your mercy, embraced with care.

While my life is guided by Your loving hands,
I'll praise You as I seek to know Your plans.

May 25
WALK IN CONFIDENCE

*What we see now is like a dim image in a mirror; then we shall see
face-to-face. What I know now is only partial; then it will be
complete—as complete as God's knowledge of me.*
1 Corinthians 13:12 (GNT)

Lord, to know You more, my soul longs after.
You give Your true peace and joyful laughter.

As Your Spirit flows through shining so bright,
Allow me to be humble, yielding in Your sight.

Let Your reflection be what others see in me,
Lord, let Your love be shown in who I am to be.

As I bow, I leave hopes and prayers with You,
I go in faith trusting You'll guide me through.

Let my praise be a beautiful song in Your ear.
For in my heart, Your presence I hold so dear.

I walk in confidence the journey You planned,
For all I've needed is provided by Your hand.

May 26
A Witness for You

---

*In your hearts honor Christ the Lord as holy, always being
prepared to make a defense to anyone who asks you for a
reason for the hope that is in you; yet do it with
gentleness and respect.*
1 Peter 3:15 (ESV)

Lord, I wonder what You think as You look at me?
Do You smile? Is there pleasure in what You see?

I pray my heart is clean and pleasing in Your eyes,
Teach me, oh Lord, to be loving, humble and wise.

Look deep into my soul and clean out all the sin.
Lord, stop any negative from creeping slowly in.

Let Your peace flow from me to those I pass by.
And help them trust so it's You they won't deny.

Lord, help me be an encourager by things I say.
As I learn how to be a witness for You each day.

Through trials Your arms help me stand strong,
You have given me purpose and my heart a song.

May 27
On That Glorious Day

My hands also will I lift up unto thy commandments,
which I have loved; and I will meditate in thy statutes.
Psalm 119:48 (KJV)

Lord, I long to be near You to set at Your feet,
To hear Your strong voice, yet kind and sweet.

In prayer I thank You for Your love and grace.
I can only imagine a gentle smile on Your face.

Surrounded by beauty as I worship and praise,
Someday, Lord, I'll be with You in endless days.

In Your presence I will humbly sing and bow.
And see my loved ones who are with You now.

My heart is rejoicing because of You I'm free,
For on that glorious day You will call for me.

May 28
CHERISHED BEYOND ANY TREASURE

For this reason also God highly exalted Him, and bestowed
on Him the name which is above every name.
Philippians 2:9 (NASB)

My strength is in You, Lord, I trust no other way,
As Your Spirit guides me by night and every day.

Your radiance is brighter than any brilliant star,
Your name is much higher than any other by far.

Your saving grace covers all things big and small,
And You know I need You when You hear my call.

In Your presence You satisfy hunger and thirst,
Because I Love You, I will always place You first.

You are my Redeemer, Savior and precious Lord,
I'm so thankful You have forgiven and restored.

You are more valuable than any earthly pleasure,
And cherished far beyond any riches or treasure.

May 29
I AM YOUR CHILD

Therefore be imitators of God, as beloved children.
Ephesians 5:1 (ESV)

Lord, grant me a heart that responds in gentle peace.
When winds of trial rage, I will trust in You to cease.

A deeper relationship with You is all I care to seek.
Draw me near to You, Lord, for I'm tired and weak.

As I give to You my burdens and my every concern,
Lord, please teach me to listen and help me learn.

I pray for a serving spirit because I am Your child,
One like You that is truly loving, gentle, and mild.

Lord, give me a generous soul free of sin's greed.
Help me be content with only what I shall need.

May 30
LIFE'S JOURNEY

*You reveal the path of life to me; in Your presence
is abundant joy; in Your right hand are eternal pleasures.*
Psalm 16:11 (HCSB)

Lord, I'll trust in whatever I must go through.
Life's journey is only about walking with You.

You are the solid Rock on which I firmly stand,
You are the giver of breath to all by Your hand.

I will trust for You always know the best way,
As I humbly ask Your Spirit to guide me, I pray.

You teach about brokenness and how You heal,
About joy, mercy, and forgiveness that is real.

Your love is that of no other I have ever known.
And peace comforts as Your presence is shown.

Thank You, Lord, for being my steadfast shield,
By teaching to grow in faith and how to yield.

May 31
I Seek Rest in Your Presence

"And if you believe, you will receive whatever you ask in prayer."
Matthew 21:22 (CSB)

Father, every moment I'm with You, I truly savor,
Make my faith strong so it won't shake or waiver.

When I look close in the mirror, what might I see?
I wonder what exists that others will find in me.

Let there be warmth in my smile and not a frown,
Help me see others in need when they feel down.

Please make my deeds gentle with the words I say,
Help me to forgive when plans do not go my way.

Lord, You know my heart for You're the One I seek,
You're my comfort and strength in times I'm weak.

I seek rest in Your presence as I journey through,
Lord, I thank You for allowing me to lean on You.

June

June 1

LORD, WITH LOVE I PRAISE YOU

O come, let us worship and bow down;
let us kneel before the LORD our Maker.
Psalm 95:6 (KJV)

Lord, with love I praise as I come here to kneel,
You are my Comforter and know just how I feel.

As I linger in the stillness of this star filled night,
Your peace reminds me the trials will be all right.

Lord, You've shown brokenness can be restored.
You are the One who is to be praised and adored.

I will not worry over fears that lie in front of me,
For You calm them all as You did the raging sea.

I'm assured You hear me when Your name I call,
Thank You for listening to prayers, big and small.

June 2

THE DEPTH OF YOUR HEART

Trust in and rely confidently on the LORD with all your heart and do not rely on your own insight or understanding.
Proverbs 3:5 (AMP)

Lord, days seem so busy with many demands.
But as I come to You, I find rest in Your hands.

My earthly vision is limited but You can see all,
I'm grateful for peace, as strength seems to fall.

Lord, if only I could see the depth of Your heart.
Yet in dreams I can't imagine the smallest part.

There's nothing in this world worth losing You,
Lord, help me stay close while I travel through.

One day Heaven will be my home, a divine place,
As we're covered by Your love and saving grace.

Life's journey with You has never been a regret,
Thank You for mercy and freely paying my debt.

June 3
SONGS OF HEAVEN

The heavens declare the glory of God,
and the sky proclaims the work of His hands.
Psalm 19:1 (HCSB)

It is a beautiful day, Lord, because You are here.
Your presence holds all things precious and dear.

As the sunrise expresses an image of Your smile,
The artistic sunsets display color for many a mile.

The warmth of Your beauty paints joy on my face,
As You trim clusters of clouds with glorious lace.

While delicate life comes forth in all living things,
Lord, it's because of goodness Your hand brings.

In divine plans we will spend eternity with You,
And when we arrive, You'll welcome us through.

Your blessings are amazing, breathtaking scenes.
As songs of Heaven replay joyfully in my dreams.

June 4

A DREAM OF HOME

By wisdom a house is built,
and by understanding it is established;
Proverbs 24:3 (ESV)

Lord, fill my home with Your presence, refusing fear,
Let Your light shine through to reveal You are here.

Open up the windows, allowing Your Spirit to flow in.
Removing any area of darkness and every inch of sin.

Each room I'd like painted with swirls of joy and love,
Adorned with peace, coming from Your hand above.

The cozy table pleasingly set for You to be seated first,
All the cups filled with grace so we will never thirst.

A sign on the door says, "Welcome, please come in",
For the one who lives here knows Jesus from within.

The lawn is planted with life's beauty bowing to You,
And nothing would ever fade as faith would renew.

My garden would flourish with all fruits of the Spirit,
For goodness and kindness grows in the midst of it.

June 5
ONLY ETERNAL HOPE

Blessed be the God and Father of our Lord Jesus Christ!
According to his great mercy, he has caused us to be born
again to a living hope through the resurrection
of Jesus Christ from the dead.
1 Peter 1:3 (ESV)

Lord, when I am with You I will never be afraid,
I think of Your sacrifice and how You freely paid.

As we surrender to You, our lives will be changed,
Life is clay in Your hands You mold and arrange.

You are the Sovereign One and only eternal hope,
In this journey with You, there is strength to cope.

When I'm in Your presence, I am safe and secure,
No one will take You away, this I know for sure.

In walking through the desert times I will survive,
You nourish my soul with joy, for in You I'm alive.

June 6
As I Journey into the Purpose

Lead me in the path of your commandments,
for I delight in it.
Psalm 119:35 (ESV)

Lord, I come before You to say; I want to follow You.
I know Your mighty hand always brings me through.

You have parted the waters revealing Your great will,
And provided rivers in the desert where life is still.

I praise You for the grace I have seen through tears.
Oh, how You have walked with me for all the years.

Lord, no fierce storm is too large for You to handle.
And no foot will ever compare to wear Your sandal.

My heart smiles because You watch us from above,
As joy overflows with thankfulness for Your love.

Lord, as I journey into the purpose designed for me.
Let Your glorious light shine to reflect only Thee.

June 7
LET MY LIFE BE A REFLECTION

We can be mirrors that brightly reflect the glory of the Lord.
And as the Spirit of the Lord works within us,
we become more and more like him.
2 Corinthians 3:18 (TLB)

Lord, You're everything precious, good and true,
When weariness clouds my vision, I look to You.

As I call out Your name You will always be there,
For I sense in Your presence how much You care.

Your promise of grace comforts and sets me free,
When I stumble and fall, You're here to rescue me.

You know my need when strength begins to sway,
When I am weak, Your eyes will never turn away.

I pledge my heart to You for as long as I shall live.
When You ask me to serve, show me how to give.

Lord, let my life be a reflection to mirror Your love,
As You guide my journey from Your throne above.

June 8
WINGS OF PROTECTION

The LORD is good, a stronghold in the day of trouble;
he knows those who take refuge in him.
Nahum 1:7 (ESV)

Lord, plant Your Word deep into my heart.
Let it refine and flourish into every part.

With Your truth and courage as my shield,
I'll trust in You, Lord, help my will to yield.

In trials You have taught me how to grow,
Much closer to You than I could ever know.

I recognize Your faithfulness is on display,
In times of quiet, I listen for what You say.

In bitter storms, Your presence gives peace,
As wings of protection make my trials cease.

June 9
MOST PERFECT TREASURE

Great is our Lord and mighty in power;
his understanding has no limit.
Psalm 147:5 (NIV)

Every time I see the Cross, Lord, I think of You,
Yet with deep suffering you carried it through.

You came from Heaven, leaving all Your glory,
With hope and grace shared in Your life story.

Your presence reflects strength within our soul,
While You mend all hearts, to make them whole.

Our future doesn't match what was in the past,
For You've planned our eternity to always last.

When hearts are hurt by sorrow and despair,
Lord, we are not alone; You are always there.

You are so worthy, our most perfect treasure.
You have mighty power far beyond measure.

June 10

Walking Through Trials

For I, the LORD your God, hold your right hand;
It is I who say to you, "Fear not, I am the one who helps you."
Isaiah 41:13 (ESV)

Lord, Your presence is real, even if sight is unclear.
As trials cloud our vision, I know You are still here.

The dark valleys and detours bring us closer to you.
We may feel the way is lost, but You see us through.

Sometimes the path is one we would never choose,
Yet as we seek You, whatever comes, we can't lose.

We need to hold tight to Your strong, steady hand.
For walking through trials may be as You planned.

Some pain may remain for a lifetime of endurance,
But we always have Your love and firm assurance.

June 11
YOUR CHILD IN HUMBLE PRAYER

*"I will be a father to you, and you will be sons
and daughters to Me", says the Lord Almighty.
2 Corinthians 6:18 (HCSB)*

Lord, I'm here as Your child in humble prayer.
I give You my trials because I know You care.

I imagine Your arms around me, big and strong,
And when frightened, You hold me all day long.

As I picture myself climbing upon Your knees,
I think of Your grace, how You hear my pleas.

I laugh at silly things for sometimes life is fun,
And shed many tears when trials have begun.

Lord, many creations You made for us to see.
I pretend You planned them especially for me.

My heart is filled with joy for You are the best,
And I am thankful because in You I find rest.

June 12

GOD, YOU ARE

The LORD is gracious and righteous;
Our God is full of compassion.
Psalm 116:5 (NIV)

God, You are the provider for every living thing.
You send rain, sunshine and cause birds to sing.

You are grace to the sinner, strength to the weak.
You restore the sick for Your healing we will seek.

You are hope to the broken, mending the heart.
You are the Divine Creator from life's very start.

You are peace in this life for everything we need.
You are the One that saves us from sinful greed.

You are the solid foundation on which we stand.
You win our battles with one raise of Your hand.

You are faith while walking in trials and wrath.
You give eternal life as we journey on our path.

June 13
AS I LOOK TO HEAVEN

*As we wait for the blessed Day we hope for, when the glory
of our great God and Savior Jesus Christ will appear.*
Titus 2:13 (GNT)

Father, thank You for the colorful beauty I see.
As I ponder the flowers, birds, and every tree.

To accept these blessings without praising You,
It would be ungrateful, Lord, I never want to do.

As I look to Heaven and picture how it will be,
I see You and loved one's waiting there for me.

The majestic reflections of red, yellow and blue,
Reminds me of Your love always faithfully true.

Often I dream of pearly gates with open doors,
And walkways of glass and shimmering floors.

I imagine clouds appearing as pillars in the sky,
With crystal stepping-stones leading up high.

Lord, I love the awesome sights here on earth.
But there's more waiting with far more worth.

June 14
WARS ARE BATTLED AND WON

Consider it pure joy, my brothers and sisters,
whenever you face trials of many kinds.
James 1:2 (NIV)

Lord, no matter what we need within every hour.
You're always here with all dominion and power.

In our prayers we can leave the pain and strife,
By trusting in You makes the difference in life.

As morning comes Your peace births new light,
And in dark times Your grace renews our sight.

I'm amazed how You calm storms within a soul,
With restless nights weary, slowly taking a toll.

Lord, in You all our wars are battled and won.
For all strength is found in You, the Holy One.

June 15
LET MY THOUGHTS GIVE GLORY

*"Then you will call on me and come and pray to me,
and I will hear you."*
Jeremiah 29:12 (RSV)

Lord, I'm thankful at Your feet trials I can lay,
As I come to kneel in humbled prayer today.

All the times I've prayed I know You've heard,
For peace comes in reading Your Holy Word.

Sometimes I hesitate asking a minor request,
Yet when I give it all to You, then I have rest.

There are days I wonder where I should begin,
But You know my heart and concerns within.

Lord, let my thoughts give glory to only You,
Because Your faithfulness brings me through.

I know all of life is held firmly in Your hands.
And answers come in Your purpose and plans.

June 16
LORD, YOU KNOW MY HEART

With my whole heart have I sought Thee:
O let me not wander from Thy commandments
Psalm 119:10 (KJV)

Lord, I will trust You, I am secure in Your sight.
For even darkness cannot dim Your divine light.

When I am frightened, I run to Your loving arms,
Shadows disappear, for there are no more harms.

Often vision is blinded, Lord, answers I can't see,
But in my spirit, I know You are always with me.

Hurt and uncertainty I have silently held inside,
Yet with You, Lord, I found I can always confide.

You are my strength I'm promised this is true,
Trials I cannot endure if I take my eyes off You.

Lord, You know my heart and depth of my love.
You are my hope and sweet Savior from above.

June 17
Lord, Guide Us in Your Will

*"I tell you the truth, those who listen to my message and believe
in God who sent me have eternal life. They will never be condemned
for their sins, but they have already passed from death into life."*
John 5:24 (NLT)

One of these days, Lord, You will come again.
We don't know the time or won't know when.

It'll be a glorious sight and wonderful vision,
I pray those waiting choose the right decision.

Your Spirit tugs souls, wanting to come inside.
Lord, draw those who are living in sinful pride.

Allow them time in giving their hearts to You,
For in Your goodness, Your promises are true.

Thank You for being our God of saving grace.
Someday we'll go home to our heavenly place.

Until then, Lord, guide us in doing Your will,
Help us in the valleys and climbing every hill.

June 18
MAKE ME PURE IN HEART

Create in me a clean heart, O God,
and renew a right spirit within me.
Psalm 51:10 (KJV)

Lord, allow Your desire to be the only thing I see.
As I dwell in Your Word, let it come to life in me.

Mold by Your Holy Spirit, make me pure in heart,
Look deep into this vessel and change every part.

Lift my faith, Lord, whenever peace seems to fade,
You are my foundation, for in You all hope is made.

Let Your light shine through Your heart to mine,
In reflecting Your goodness and steadfast design.

Lord, on this journey help me walk without fear,
Because every day it is You, I will seek to be near.

June 19
SWEET GRACE IS MINE

Let us come boldly unto the throne of grace, that
we may obtain mercy, and find grace to help in time of need.
Hebrews 4:16 (KJV)

Lord, help me glorify You every step I make,
As my praise honors You, each breath I take.

To be in Your presence brings joy to my soul,
In You, I have peace for You make me whole.

You promised mercy and sweet grace is mine.
As I trust in You, Lord, life is all in Your time.

Guide me by Your Spirit, Your Word I receive.
Your hope gives strength and in You, I believe.

I worship You for being my Savior and Lord,
I am grateful because my life's been restored.

June 20
REFUGE IN YOU

How precious is Your mercy, God!
And the sons of mankind take refuge
in the shadow of Your wings.
Psalm 36:7 (NASB)

Lord, there's no one that will ever compare to You.
You are the light in darkness guiding me through.

The pain You were caused from all the earthly sin,
You bore on Your shoulders to give us life again.

The thoughts of Your sacrifice humbles my heart.
For You carried our iniquities from the very start.

I am so thankful You watch over me from above,
And so very grateful for Your abundant true love.

As I yearn for Your presence in the morning still,
Lord, I'll take refuge in You as I abide in Your will.

June 21

WITHOUT DARKNESS STARS CAN'T SHINE BRIGHT

Blessed is the man who endures temptation;
for when he has been approved, he will receive the crown of life
which the Lord has promised to those who love Him.
James 1:12 (NKJV)

Lord, You mold tears into gratitude and laughter,
And through trials there is always a rainbow after.

Sometimes struggles come to help us see the light,
For without the darkness, stars can't shine bright.

You are truly matchless and I honor You, my Lord,
As my strength and peace, You are greatly adored.

Without You my heart would be sad and broken,
Yet I'll never be alone, for Your Word has spoken.

I love You, Lord, for in You I am humbly blessed,
To be wrapped in Your arms, I am always at rest.

June 22

YOUR PRESENCE IS MY SAFE PLACE

And He said, "My presence shall go with thee,
and I will give thee rest."
Exodus 33:14 (KJV)

As I watched the quiet rain falling from the sky,
Soft clouds were slowly changing way up high.

Lord, how I long to glorify Your awesome name,
In looking to Heaven, I'm blessed why You came.

While I worship You, Lord, through all my days,
I'll rise above earthly trials to give You praise.

When I come to You to restore my thirsty soul,
The closeness I receive makes my heart whole.

Amid the darkness, Your light breaks through.
And I live for moments, I have glimpses of You.

I'll rest in Your presence, for it is my safe place.
There I find peace and joy with forgiving grace.

June 23
PRAYERS I LAY AT YOUR FEET

Lead me in Your truth and teach me,
For You are the God of my salvation;
On You I wait all the day long.
Psalm 25:5 (NKJV)

Lord, in my prayer I come before Your throne,
For You are my Father and my heart You own.

I feel Your voice but I'm uncertain what to do,
Please give guidance as I desire to follow You.

Strengthen my faith as I walk a path I can't see,
Lord, direct my life as You would have it to be.

You're my anchor of hope to help me through,
And if fears arise, draw my eyes back to You.

You know my prayers I lay them at Your feet,
For I trust and long for the day we will meet.

June 24
PEACE BEYOND FULL MEASURE

And the effect of righteousness will be peace,
and the result of righteousness, quietness and trust forever.
Isaiah 32:17 (ESV)

My soul praises You, Lord, for everything You are to me.
You removed the brokenness that no one else could see.

I pledge my heart with love throughout all tomorrows,
You transform trials to blessings with no more sorrows.

It is in Your goodness You brought me gently through,
Every moment in our special place, I am closer to You.

You melted away all worry as fear was replaced by joy,
You granted renewed hope; the enemy tried to destroy.

You give peace that overwhelms beyond full measure,
For the promises from You are my priceless treasure.

Thank You, Lord, I'll always worship Your Holy Name,
Oh, how my life has changed, I will forever proclaim!

June 25
Trust Found in You

Taste and see that the LORD is good.
Oh, the joys of those who take refuge in him!
Psalm 34:8 (NLT)

Living life together, Lord, is all I desire to do,
Every day is better while I spend it with You.

I'll listen for Your whisper as You speak to me.
While You brighten my path, You help me see.

Lord, let my words bring honor to You each day.
Help me to walk by faith as You guide my way.

You are everything to me, Lord, that will matter.
For all those earthly treasures, break or shatter.

My trust, found in only You, I'll forever rejoice,
As I rest in the comfort of Your heavenly voice.

June 26
EVERY MOUNTAIN I CLIMB

He gives power to the weak,
And to those who have no might He increases strength.
Isaiah 40:29 (NKJV)

Lord, my eyes shall see You someday in Your glory.
While I praise You for being author of my life story.

As I walk through the days with You on my mind,
I think about Your goodness, how gentle and kind.

Every mountain I climb I will draw closer to You,
Your presence keeps me strong in everything I do.

I thank You, Lord, for lessons taught through strife,
How You have never left me alone anytime in life.

No matter what comes my way, I am truly blessed,
I'll always lean on You, Lord, for in You I can rest.

June 27
TEACH ME TO FOLLOW YOUR WILL

Teach me your way, O LORD;
I will walk in Your truth;
Unite my heart to fear Your name.
Psalm 86:11 (NKJV)

Lord, I just want to talk to You again today.
I love my time with You more than I can say.

I'll praise how You mended my broken heart,
And how I need You directing in every part.

Lord, as I wait on You, I promise to be still.
And as I walk, teach me to follow Your will.

To live without You I wouldn't want to do,
Thank You for helping me make it through.

In weary days, I'm glad You're always here,
Trusting in You erases all my worldly fear.

June 28

CHANGED THROUGH IT ALL

---

*I will give you a new heart and put a new spirit in you;
I will remove from you your heart of stone and
give you a heart of flesh.
Ezekiel 36:26 (NIV)*

Lord, I want to bring honor, to do what is right.
Let my praise be exalted in Your divine sight.

You mend brokenness with Your power to heal,
And give sweet peace the enemy cannot steal.

When we give You our shameful sin and strife,
You create a clean heart to start a renewed life.

In Your seasons, we are changed through it all,
As souls are saved through Your Spirit's call.

Life is a measurement of time as Your planned,
You know each detail, it's all in Your command.

June 29
The Palm of Your Hand

See, I have engraved you on the palms of my hands;
your walls are ever before me.
Isaiah 49:16 (NIV)

Lord, as I think how much You mean to me.
I know without You my security wouldn't be.

For You God, I rejoice placing my trust in You,
As gratefulness fills my heart for all You do.

I will look upon You giving honor and praise,
As I thank You for Your mercies all of my days.

I cannot fathom the depth of Your divine love,
Yet thankful You take care of me from above.

I'm humbled my name is written on Your hand,
And someday soon in Your presence I'll stand.

June 30
THE HEM OF YOUR GARMENT

"Blessed are they which do hunger and thirst after righteousness:
for they shall be filled."
Matthew 5:6 (KJV)

Lord, I need peace, just to be alone with You to talk.
As I close my eyes, I imagine sharing a quiet walk.

I believe You are leading me along a path I can't see,
A way unknown, yet I trust where You're taking me.

You show grace to broken hearts, teaching to forgive,
Giving courage to accept change as we learn to live.

You helped me see blessings in sorrow and healings,
As You restored my spirit from many hurt feelings.

Lord, help me touch the hem of Your garment today.
I know Your Spirit hears my words each time I pray.

I love You, there's nothing more beautiful than You,
Lord, I thank You from my heart for all that You do.

July

July 1
WE LEARN TO TRUST

And this small and temporary trouble we suffer will bring us a tremendous and eternal glory, much greater than the trouble.
2 Corinthians 4:17 (GNT)

God, You are the answer to heart's deepest requests,
Yet sometimes we must endure tribulation and tests.

You've planned life in ways to help us get stronger,
As we gain patience in delays while waiting longer.

In times of weakness, faith brings us closer to You,
Because of Your strength, we can make it through.

As we try to understand, often there is not a choice,
Yet aware it's for our good, we listen to Your voice.

When we walk through trials, Your mercies are just.
As we lean on Your Word, it is then we learn to trust.

July 2
I'll Follow Where You Lead

*The LORD guides us in the way we should go
and protects those who please him.
Psalms 37:23 (GNT)*

Lord, when I think of the sad prayers You hear,
I know You hold troubled hearts and every tear.

I can't imagine the burdens cast on You each day,
Or how Your heart breaks as we wander or stray.

As You strengthen our faith with renewed hope,
We lean on Your promise, giving courage to cope.

I thank You for listening to all my many prayers.
As I trust You, Lord, I believe You bear my cares.

You've been faithful to me through so much pain,
You have removed brokenness and every chain.

I am so grateful, Lord, for You provide all I need.
As I walk Your ways, I will follow where You lead.

July 3
YOU WALK WITH ME THERE

Walk in obedience to all that the LORD your God has commanded you, so that you may live and prosper and prolong your days in the land that you will possess.
Deuteronomy 5:33 (NIV)

Lord, my soul is filled with joy because of who You are,
Your brilliance shines brighter than any heavenly star.

I am thankful, Lord, for Your answers to humble prayer,
No matter where my path leads, You walk with me there.

I long to stay in Your presence praising and loving You,
My heart is grateful for this place You've brought me to.

Your plans have been unknown walking along my way,
I trust You know my thoughts as I come to You to pray.

Lord, You've given me a peace that only You can know.
This journey is uncertain, Lord, but I'm not afraid to go.

July 4
ALL THINGS ARE POSSIBLE

*And without faith it is impossible to please him, for whoever
would draw near to God must believe that he exists and
that he rewards those who seek him.*
Hebrews 11:6 (ESV)

Lord, our souls become beautiful because of You,
When filled with Your grace, hearts are made new.

How You work in mysterious ways only You know,
We are unworthy, yet Your love You always show.

Through trials You give strength so we can stand.
But sometimes we are tested and sifted like sand.

All things are possible, You break chains within,
For salvation in You removes the weight of sin.

As hearts are molded by Your goodness and love,
Peace and joy are blessings granted from above.

July 5
NAIL SCARRED HAND

He heals the brokenhearted, and binds up their wounds.
Psalm 147:3 (RSV)

Lord, You are the highest treasure of worth,
Yet much is wasted on many things on earth.

Those desperate souls need You to find hope,
While seeking Your presence and how to cope.

They search for someone to listen and to care,
Harboring many problems too difficult to bear.

Within all the trials, You draw us closer to you,
Blessing us with peace as we journey through.

As your grace mends wounds by day and night,
You fill our souls with strength, renewing sight.

Lord, help those believe as You have planned.
When hearts reach for Your nail scarred hand.

July 6
ANSWERS ARE HELD IN YOUR HAND

The LORD who created you says, "Do not be afraid—I will
save you. I have called you by name—you are mine."
Isaiah 43:1 (GNT)

While raindrops cover my face, I breathe in fresh air,
As I am thinking about You, Lord, and how You care.

When my vision is blurred, You always provide sight,
Even in darkness, Your presence is my guiding light.

In every trial, You've faithfully promised to be near.
For in Your mercy, You never fail to wipe every tear.

Lord, my soul whispers, there's no hope without You,
For we need Your gentle peace to carry us through.

Our troubles You know as countless grains of sand,
But we trust You, as answers are held in Your hand.

July 7
IN YOUR DIVINE GOODNESS

He who conceals his transgressions will not prosper,
but he who confesses and forsakes them will obtain mercy.
Proverbs 28:13 (RSV)

Lord, Your sweet presence fills my soul with peace,
As joy overflows removing fear and troubles cease.

You quietly bless our time together how I need it so,
I'm not sure what to say, but just want you to know.

I will always desire to praise You for my entire life,
And thank You for helping through trials and strife.

Lord, I am so undeserving yet Your mercies I see,
My heart is grateful because You have loved me.

It is in Your divine goodness all trials take place,
Yet through Your love, we receive eternal grace.

Draw me nearer, Lord, I want to know You more,
Just to feel Your presence more than ever before.

July 8
Tomorrow Is Uncertain

The LORD will give strength unto his people;
The LORD will bless his people with peace.
Psalm 29:11 (KJV)

As I hear tranquil sounds in the evening's light,
I sit comforted by Your sweet Spirit in the night.

Lord, I'll give you praise for Your goodness I see,
I don't deserve blessings You've bestowed on me.

How I've grown to love You much more each day,
While I am drawn closer as we walk on our way.

Lord, my heart is yours You can see through it all.
I will always trust in You, help me hear Your call.

Tomorrow is uncertain, yet it rests in Your hands.
For life's path is designed by Your divine plans.

July 9
GRACE PAID THE WAY

Grace, mercy, peace shall be with us, from God the Father,
and from Jesus Christ, the Son of the Father, in truth and love.
2 John 1:3 (ASV)

Lord, Your presence is revealed in wonderful ways.
I love the assurance You are with us all of our days.

In the most precious place of my heart, I hold You,
I'm so thankful You're in my life each day through.

I see You in the fragrant flowers, so soft and sweet,
And in smiles of friendly faces, I pass on the street.

Peace and joy were found the day our hearts met,
For Your grace paid the way to forgive all my debt.

I'm happy You've planned my life where I'm to go,
My trust is in You, Lord, because I cherish You so.

Lord, I ask You to take my hand; I want You to lead.
You are my God and always give more than I need.

July 10
HEAVEN AND EARTH WILL BOW

*"You, LORD, you alone are LORD; you made the heavens
and the stars of the sky. You made land and sea and
everything in them; you gave life to all. The heavenly
powers bow down and worship you.*
Nehemiah 9:6 (GNT)

God, You are the Creator of every living thing.
Even tiny birds You gave a soft voice to sing.

You know each grain on the warm sandy beach,
And You number all the stars far out of reach.

You designed every fiber for our heart to beat,
As we trust in You, lives are made complete.

All of Heaven and earth will bow down to You,
As we praise the One so faithful and true.

Our blessings are gifts from Your hands above,
All because You give of Your divine love.

July 11
THROUGH YOUR EYES

I will instruct you and teach you in the way you should go;
I will counsel you with my eye on you.
Psalm 32:8 (RSV)

Lord, humble my heart as I come to You in prayer,
Search my soul within to see all that dwells there.

Make me one that hungers, Your Word I will seek,
Through all the testing, especially when I'm weak.

If I could look through Your eyes to what You see,
My hope is Your heart would be pleased with me.

I cherish moments with You I've cried and talked,
For You are faithful on this journey I have walked.

With every sunrise, I want to draw closer to You,
I'll always need You, Lord, to guide me through.

Thank You for grace and the blessings I have had.
I will be fully devoted in good times and the sad.

July 12
BLANKET OF PROVISION

*It is he who will supply all your needs from his riches
in glory because of what Christ Jesus has done for us.
Philippians 4:19 (TLB)*

Lord, thank You for always listening when I pray,
You hear every word, even the ones I forget to say.

I'm grateful for the love You have always shown,
Your presence is all I need, I'll never walk alone.

My journey is planned where I'm destined to be,
Your timing is whatever You would have for me.

You've always been faithful to carry me through,
Everything I have needed You provided that too.

Your blanket of provision will always be enough,
Even during the trials when life seems so tough.

July 13
A Sight to Behold

For God, who said, "Let there be light in the darkness,"
has made us understand that it is the brightness of his
glory that is seen in the face of Jesus Christ.
2 Corinthians 4:6 (TLB)

Father, I dream about spending eternity with You.
I would love to sit at Your feet every day through.

My sincere devotion to every word You would say,
Will be endless time together where I want to stay.

All cares will be left behind with no more worry,
There would be no more reason to rush or hurry.

Every tear and pain will be forever swept away,
With joy filled hearts we'll praise You every day.

Majestic angels in worship, such a sight to behold,
As we walk into Heaven, welcomed to Your fold.

July 14
I Adore You, Lord

I love Thee, O LORD, my strength.
Psalm 18:1 (KJV)

Do I love You, Lord? Do I fully trust You?
You know my heart, I honestly and truly do.

My desire is to follow as You faithfully lead.
Your name gives grace, nothing more I need.

I'll praise You forever in eternity I will live,
You're worthy of much more than I can give.

I am grateful how You always care for me,
How You've blessed for things I cannot see.

Lord, I've given all my heart, soul and mind,
And as I glorify You, all fear is left behind.

I adore You, Lord, far more than I can say.
Your kindness amazes me every single day.

July 15
THE JOURNEY

And this world is fading away, and these evil
forbidden things will go with it, but whoever
keeps doing the will of God will live forever.
1 John 2:17 (TLB)

Hold my hand, Lord, as we walk through this day.
The journey is Yours I trust You'll show the way.

When I become weak hold me so I don't stumble,
Help me lean on You, always remaining humble.

When trials are difficult and begin to take toll,
You lead me to quiet refuge comforting my soul.

There's no path I can go that You have not seen,
If I'm walking the wrong way, please intervene.

Help me know Your heart and follow Your will,
Lord, show me where to go and when to be still.

July 16
NEVER ANOTHER SAD TEAR

But our citizenship is in heaven. And we eagerly await
a Savior from there, the Lord Jesus Christ.
Philippians 3:20 (NIV)

Someday we'll be leaving to go with You precious Lord,
At that time our old bodies will be healed and restored.

Heaven I envision to be a glorious and awesome sight,
It will be a wonderful day, for there will never be night.

You designed a perfect home with no comparison here,
There is no reason to worry or give over to earthly fear.

The wonders of Heaven will be such beauty for our eyes,
With all of Your creation, adorned by spectacular skies.

You will come to meet us as we kneel in humble praise.
We'll worship and honor You, Lord, the rest of our days.

As You welcome us, we'll never shed another sad tear.
Lord Jesus, I am overjoyed for the awaited day is near.

July 17
WHAT WOULD I DO WITHOUT YOU?

Give thanks to the LORD, for He is good;
His faithful love endures forever.
Psalm 118:1 (HCSB)

As I gaze up to Heaven, Lord, my focus is on You,
I am reminded You're not far but near in all I do.

I love to drift away in Your presence I find peace,
It is here I feel joy and my burdens begin to cease.

There's security in this place I don't want to leave,
Your Spirit softly whispers, Your mercy I receive.

As I think of the past filled with the unsure days,
And how You changed my life in awesome ways.

I'll praise You, Lord, and thank You for loving me.
What would I do without You? Where would I be?

July 18
While Waiting on You, Lord

*But if we hope for what we do not see, we wait eagerly
for it with patience and composure.*
Romans 8:25 (AMP)

Lord, as I kneel in this quiet place where I find You,
I rest in silence for I need You to help me through.

I am no one special but my heart You always see,
I thank You for times You have watched over me.

Teach me to follow in Your ways, giving up mine,
While on this journey, I pray let Your light shine.

All times I prayed, You have removed my fears,
Giving peace in trials, brushing away my tears.

When I seek You my need is to know You more,
And I have learned to trust for what is in store.

While waiting on You, Lord, I desire Your will,
As You move mountains I'll continue to be still.

July 19
MY GOD OF PEACE

I have set the LORD continually before me;
Because He is at my right hand, I will not be shaken.
Psalm 16:8 (NASB)

Sometimes I struggle in finding my way through,
Yet Lord, the unknown paths lead directly to You.

When hearts are broken, feeling defeated by pain,
You bless us with divine peace, Your joy we gain.

Only You, Lord, hold power and strength to cope,
Nothing more on this earth can give us true hope.

As I call on You, Your Holy Spirit draws me near,
Prayers are not lost but go straight to Your ear.

I pray for permission to see through Your eyes.
By asking You, Lord, my faith continues to rise.

You are my God of peace watching from on high,
I'll give You praise as You draw Your child nigh.

July 20
SPRING OF ABUNDANT HOPE

Therefore my heart is glad and my whole being rejoices;
my body also rests securely.
Psalm 16:9 (CSB)

Lord, as I rise early to give You honor and praise,
Your goodness gives joy to my heart in all ways.

You lead me to a peaceful place with love and care.
As sure as the new dawn, You are always there.

You hear even my whisper when I share my heart,
You know all my concerns, even the smallest part.

I will drink from Your spring of abundant hope,
As You prepare my soul for the strength to cope.

My life has been changed by Your inspired Word,
In trusting You, my prayers are faithfully heard.

July 21
The Good Shepherd

And now just as you trusted Christ to save you, trust him, too,
for each day's problems; live in vital union with him.
Colossians 2:6 (TLB)

Reign in my life, Lord, I want to soak in all of You,
Let Your Holy Spirit cover me in everything I do.

I long to be in Your presence, my peaceful place.
Just to imagine love and joy shown on Your face.

In wilderness You have never once forgotten me,
And in trials, You opened my eyes so I could see.

When in valleys, I learned to fix my sight on You,
It is there I am reminded You bring me through.

You are the Good Shepherd, guide us Your way,
Lord, I'll need You walking with me every day.

July 22
ANSWERS COME AT APPOINTED TIMES

*But forget not this one thing, beloved, that one day is with
the Lord as a thousand years, and a thousand years as one day.*
2 Peter 3:8 (ASV)

Lord, I thank You for provisions in this world I live,
I'm so grateful for all I see in the blessings You give.

Even if the journey is filled with turmoil and wrath,
Your Holy Spirit quietly guides and protects my path.

It's amazing how You planned for every single hour,
As our chains are broken by Your renewing power.

You tell us to trust, be strong and do not be afraid,
Your mercy outweighs actions we carelessly made.

In earthly prayers, we often want them all our way,
Yet Your reply may be in silence or for another day.

Lord, as I listen for direction, let me patiently wait.
For answers come at appointed times, never late.

July 23
MY SAFE PLACE

God is our refuge and strength, a very present help in trouble.
Psalm 46:1 (KJV)

I come to honor You, God, I'm humbled as I pray,
You see how I love and need You more each day.

While my soul longs for You all praise will flow,
For in prayer, Lord, my heart You always know.

In my safe place, I am comforted by Your side.
Those times I lose the way, You are my guide.

When I walk through a test, You hold my hand,
As You draw close for You always understand.

I feel sweet peace as we share time together,
And during the storm, I know we can weather.

Thank You, Lord, for love and forgiving grace.
Every time I'm weak, I come to seek Your face.

July 24
MADE FOR YOUR PURPOSE

We now have this light shining in our hearts, but we ourselves are like fragile clay jars containing this great treasure. This makes it clear that our great power is from God, not from ourselves.
2 Corinthians 4:7 (NLT)

Lord, let not my heart grow callous, mold it like clay.
Help me hear Your whisper of every word You say.

I submit to the shaping and kneading of Your hands,
To be made for Your purpose, fashioned to Your plans.

In times of brokenness, when strength seems to leave,
You are always renewing my faith to help me believe.

You've granted peace in valleys I haven't understood.
Yet I learned to trust as the bad was turned to good.

Your blessings are abundant, thank You for my trials,
Even if You're silent, it doesn't always mean denials.

Lord, mold me to be a vessel filled totally with You.
To feel Your Spirit overflowing in all I need to do.

July 25
True Promises of Hope

---

*"But those who drink the water I give will never be thirsty again.
It becomes a fresh, bubbling spring within them,
giving them eternal life."*
John 4:14 (NLT)

Lord, I need Your mercy and peace surrounding me.
To overcome all daily trials only Your eyes can see.

While living in this life, Lord, help me to stay strong.
No matter the journey, I will sing You a praise song.

Lord, pour into me refreshing water only You bring.
I'm here to drink again from Your abundant spring.

As I meet those in my path with a bleeding heart,
Help me share how You offer a brand new start.

There is nothing I know You can't ever make new,
We have true promises of hope found only in You.

July 26
OUR MIGHTY STRONGHOLD

Though I walk in the midst of trouble, You will revive me;
You will stretch out Your hand against the wrath of my enemies,
And Your right hand will save me.
Psalm 138:7 (AMP)

To You, Lord, I give my love it will never part,
I'll enter this day with praise within my heart.

The journey is peaceful with every step I take,
Even in the midst of trials and the heartache.

You are hope and joy, our mighty stronghold,
Your name is more worthy than silver or gold.

I'll honor You each day for watching over me,
For I trust in whatever You want my life to be.

Lord, I'll daily walk the path planned by You,
When I'm weak, You always help me through.

July 27
On Fertile Ground

Sow righteousness for yourselves and reap faithful love;
break up your unplowed ground. It is time to seek the LORD
until he comes and sends righteousness on you like the rain.
Hosea 10:12 (CSB)

Lord, the longing in my heart is to glorify You,
Guide me on this path as You take me through.

Plant Your Word in my soul on fertile ground.
With only Your mercy and peace to be found.

Allow Your gentleness and joy to fill my heart.
Sow seeds of Your love throughout every part.

Lord, I'm so humbled by Your blessings today.
For Your grace is mine as Your promises say.

Help me grow with nothing earthly to desire,
And honor You as the most precious I admire.

July 28
SECURE IN YOUR PRESENCE

And He said, "My Presence will go with you,
and I will give you rest."
Exodus 33:14 (NKJV)

Lord, You have known my weakness yet carry me along,
On the days my vision is dim and my strength is gone.

With tears of joy, I'm thankful You help me understand.
How You forgive when I forget You have it all planned.

Your eyes have seen the tears through pain I have felt,
You have always listened while in prayer I have knelt.

Secure in Your presence removes fear of the unknown,
Thank You for endless love and grace You have shown.

Lord, I will praise You for assurance Your Word gives,
For You know in my heart is where Your Spirit lives.

July 29
NO ONE LIKE YOU

No one is as holy as the Lord! There is no other God,
Nor any Rock like our God.
1 Samuel 2:2 (TLB)

Lord, we meet in the stillness of my heart.
As I ask You to search and mold every part.

How can I please You? Show me Your ways.
Help me in the waiting through Your delays.

Some days I have not been strong I confess,
It's then You bring me into Your arms to rest.

These moments alone I desperately long for,
As I'm drawn closer, I need You even more.

There's no one like You, nothing compares,
You are the only refuge, the One who cares.

Lord, through every moment, in all that I do.
With each breath, I will always praise You.

July 30
PRICELESS GIFTS

Let your adorning be the hidden person of the heart with the imperishable beauty of a gentle and quiet spirit, which in God's sight is very precious.
1 Peter 3:4 (ESV)

Lord, I just need to come and rest at Your feet today.
I give You reign over my concerns as I kneel to pray.

My heart is filled with gladness for it is You I serve,
I'll honor You with praise You abundantly deserve.

Grant me a tender heart full of compassion and love.
Guide me with Your favor as You watch from above.

When I am with You, my heart is happy and aglow,
Grace and joy are priceless gifts You freely bestow.

You shelter through pain from each restless night,
As Your Spirit comforts me in the midst of fright.

There is truth in Your precious name, I love You so.
I'll trust You every day for Your goodness I know.

July 31
A HEART FULL OF THANKSGIVING

I will praise you, LORD, with all my heart;
I will tell of all the wonderful things you have done.
Psalm 9:1 (GNT)

Lord, it is peaceful here spending time with You,
While the sky bursts brilliant, crimson and blue.

As I look to Heaven clouds appear as angel wings,
Reminding of Your promise and peace it brings.

The graceful swans drift with not a worry in sight,
Gliding motionless through the day into the night.

In stillness, the warm rain turned to a gentle mist,
As hummingbirds fly by flowers, they softly kissed.

Your creatures live day by day without a concern,
Yet do not understand the lessons we must learn.

When I think of the trials and every breakthrough,
I am grateful for You, a Savior so loving and true.

Lord, to praise You daily makes life worth living.
I will honor You with a heart full of thanksgiving.

August

August 1
POWER TO MOVE MOUNTAINS

"I assure you: If anyone says to this mountain, 'Be lifted up and thrown into the sea,' and does not doubt in his heart, but believes that what he says will happen, it will be done for him."
Mark 11:23 (HCSB)

Lord, in life we're overcomers with You by our side.
As we walk hand in hand, close to You as our guide.

You have given a purpose to honor and praise You,
To tell of Your love and how You bring us through.

When hearts are broken or shattered, You are there,
You cover hurt and pain with so much loving care.

You settle troubled waters tossed about by doubt,
While refreshing thirsty souls in times of drought.

You have power to move mountains when we trust,
And You calm the raging sea that lives within us.

August 2
GRACE HEALS WOUNDED HEARTS

He heals the brokenhearted and bandages their wounds.
Psalm 147:3 (CSB)

Lord, You are joy to my heart, strength to my soul.
You've shown mercy as I have given You control.

Teach me about Your love, then let me give it away.
Lord, my life belongs to You have it all Your way.

Morning after morning I will seek and worship You,
In valleys I am drawn closer as we walk through.

Your light is far brighter than all the moon and stars,
Your grace heals wounded hearts with ugly scars.

You're the beautiful sunset at the end of every day,
As I whisper Your name, You hear words I pray.

August 3
HUMBLED BY YOUR GRACE

"Blessed are the merciful, for they will receive mercy."
Matthew 5:7 (AMP)

God, I will honor You when moments of life are glad,
And praise You even in those times my heart is sad.

Your Word is a strong tower standing tall and true,
Thank You for peace while spending time with You.

When my hope fades in storms, causing loss of sight,
You faithfully bring me back guided with Your light.

Your joy proves faithfulness in hard times we share,
Your kindness is abundant with love You don't spare.

You are the One I seek daily and the One I most love.
As Your arms wrap around me from Heaven above.

Your blessings are more than I could have believed,
I am humbled by Your grace for mercy I've received.

August 4
WITH EVERY BREATH I TAKE

Be strong, and let your heart be courageous,
all you who put your hope in the LORD.
Psalm 31:24 (CSB)

Lord, my heart is troubled until I'm alone with You.
Please lead me as Your strength brings me through.

While I dwell in Your presence, a place I want to be.
I read Your Word, telling just how You care for me.

Lord, my needs are few, only to sit at Your throne.
I want to be closer to You, more than I've known.

My heart is filled with gladness of all that You are,
I'll rest in You, my Savior and maker of every star.

With every breath I take, I'll need You even more.
Lord, I'm sorry for pain You felt and sin You bore.

August 5
LIVING WATER

"He who believes in me, as the scripture has said,
'Out of his heart shall flow rivers of living water."
John 7:38 (RSV)

Lord, in those times of waiting I will trust in You,
Even when I can't see ahead You take me through.

Your Spirit dwells within me with truth and love,
You guide and watch over me from Heaven above.

You have comforted my broken and brittle heart,
And have made complete all that was torn apart.

You gently removed my pain I often locked inside,
You opened my heart, releasing what tried to hide.

You give living water as we drink from Your well,
And in Your presence, I'm happy to always dwell.

August 6
WE WILL NOT BE ALONE

My soul clings to you; Your right hand upholds me.
Psalm 63:8 (ESV)

Lord, Your Word is rich in strength and peace.
You cover us with mercy, telling trials to cease.

It is written we must walk worthy of Your call,
Yet You help when worry tries to make us fall.

When we feel stress we come to You in prayer,
It is in Your presence You show how You care.

Times we are wounded we will not be alone,
Because You never leave us to be on our own.

As I bow to worship, I humbly seek Your face,
I thank You for mercy and Your amazing grace.

August 7
WHEN THERE IS NOTHING MORE TO DO

For God gave us not a spirit of fearfulness;
but of power and love and discipline.
2 Timothy 1:7 (ASV)

Lord, You are the light in the darkest of night,
You give Your vision whenever I have no sight.

You go before me, for paths are seldom clear,
And quietly remind me, You are always here.

When there is nothing more that I know to do,
I will always set my eyes trusting only on You.

Our life may not be one we would have chose,
But You plan our journey no one else knows.

Your strength outweighs troubles of this time,
Lord, thank You, for peace I'll claim to be mine.

August 8
I Will Trust You, Lord

Commit thy way unto the LORD; trust also in him;
and he shall bring it to pass.
Psalm 37:5 (KJV)

Lord, I'm letting go of my selfish dreams,
I lay them down as tears become streams.

When I don't hear from You I will not fear,
But trust in You for I know You are near.

I've tried things my way this I will confess,
Lord, feeling tired I need to have Your rest.

Without understanding I will not ask why,
But I will trust You, Lord, as the days go by.

You've planned my future and seen my past,
You have known my prayers before I asked.

You have given peace with a steadfast hand,
You're my firm foundation on which I stand.

August 9
WHEN THERE SEEMS NO OTHER WAY

"But true wisdom and power are found in God;
counsel and understanding are his."
Job 12:13 (NLT)

Lord, I need Your strong arms securely around me.
And I desire Your guidance on this journey to be.

In Your presence, I pray and my worries are gone.
I am thankful we have You to trust and depend on.

You have seen my concerns and known all the fears.
Thank You for being faithful in wiping all my tears.

Lord, deep in my soul Your name is treasured there,
I am grateful for Your blessings and how Your care.

You make a way when there seems no other way,
For Your miracles can happen on any given day.

August 10
DRAW ME NEAR, LORD

The Lord is close to the brokenhearted;
he rescues those whose spirits are crushed.
Psalm 34:18 (NLT)

Draw me near, my Lord, I need nothing but You,
As You search in my heart, You see this is true.

Your Spirit refreshes as a gentle spring shower.
Your tender mercies renew my soul every hour.

As burdens grow weary You whisper, "Be still",
In silence, I'm reminded to listen to Your will.

In days my strength fails and I grow so weak,
I will not fear for it is You my heart will seek.

No matter what may come today or tomorrow,
I will be thankful amid the pain and sorrow.

Draw me near, Lord, so storms I can weather.
I can face trials when You and I are together.

August 11
FORGIVEN AND GLAD

---

*He is the Spirit of truth. The world is unable to receive him
because it doesn't see him or know him. But you do know him,
because he remains with you and will be in you.*
John 14:17 (CSB)

Lord, I will give all of my life trials to You,
As I walk in faith You'll bring me through.

I know You can handle far more than this,
Lord, it is in Your timing and never amiss.

Your Word says to trust You with my fear.
And Your strong hands will wipe each tear.

Your sweet Spirit guides me into all truth,
Your eyes have seen far before my youth.

I was created to love You with all my heart,
Nothing is hiding, Lord, search every part.

Those that don't know You will be very sad,
But those that do will be forgiven and glad.

August 12
EVERY MOMENT IS A BLESSING

LORD, your constant love reaches the heavens;
your faithfulness extends to the skies.
Psalm 36:5 (GNT)

Lord, I know the goodness You provide from above,
Let me live with an open heart to share Your love.

Your mercy and grace is beautiful, faithful and free,
Living in Your presence is how life is planned to be.

There is much joy in everything surrounded by You,
Every moment is a blessing as You walk me through.

Your words touch my heart and covers over my soul,
As Your Holy Spirit speaks, Heaven is made my goal.

Lord, Your hope is true and endless in this life I live,
And relentless are the promises You graciously give.

August 13
IT IS YOU, LORD

The LORD has heard my supplication;
the LORD accepts my prayer.
Psalm 6:9 (RSV)

Lord, I need time alone with You again today.
To spend moments at Your feet just to pray.

It is You, Lord, who holds me whenever I fall,
You always pick me up to help me stand tall.

It is You, Lord, who I can give my troubles to.
I trust You to show me what more I'm to do.

It is You, Lord, who listens to each word I say.
And I'm grateful You walk beside me every day.

It is You, Lord, the One and only eternal love.
Thank You for guidance from Heaven above.

It is You, Lord, who I praise when I am alone.
For I know You never leave me on my own.

August 14
WHEN STORMS OF LIFE COME

When the whirlwind passes, the wicked are no more,
but the righteous are secure forever.
Proverbs 10:25 (CSB)

Lord, let me stand firm on Your unshakable ground.
Allow no doubt in my heart anywhere to be found.

In every season, You're with me leading by Your hand.
I will faithfully trust in whatever You have planned.

When rivers of adversity are raging fierce and strong,
We are to be ready when storms of life come along.

Help me walk in Your ways and teach me to be wise.
With desire to be humble, pleasing in Your eyes.

Lord, open my ears hearing every word You will say.
While on this journey, I'll follow You every day.

Thank You for mercy found in Your peace and love.
With divine grace, You always give from above.

August 15
THE WATERS OF FAITH

---

*"And I will always guide you and satisfy you with good things.
I will keep you strong and well. You will be like a garden that has
plenty of water, like a spring of water that never goes dry."
Isaiah 58:11 (GNT)*

Lord, as I step deeper in the waters of faith in You,
Please guide with Your Spirit as I walk through.

I need You to carry me when my strength is too low.
Dwelling on You, Lord, brings joy only You know.

You are my Lord, and close to my heart, You'll stay.
For my prayers, I'll lay at Your feet day after day.

The answer to all my questions may never appear,
Yet Lord, in my heart, You will always be here.

Your faithfulness has been given abundantly to me,
And Your miracles I believe are yet to see.

Your mercies are new each day flowing from above,
You are my Redeemer; You have all of my love.

August 16
THE SONG I SING

I will sing about the LORD'S faithful love forever;
I will proclaim Your faithfulness to all generations.
Psalm 89:1 (HCSB)

Lord, I want to tell you how much You mean to me.
And I'm thankful because You've set my spirit free.

I will praise You for miracles throughout my story,
For all blessings flow from Your throne in Glory.

When You remove our stains, clothing us in white,
Your Spirit leads in the days and protects by night.

You washed my soul with joy, leaving no sorrow,
As You guide, I'll walk through every tomorrow.

You are the song I sing and the fresh air I receive.
Every day has new hope because of You, I believe.

August 17
I Lift Your Name Up High

For I am not ashamed of the gospel, because it is the power
of God that brings salvation to everyone who believes ...
Romans 1:16 (NIV)

Lord, show me Your path as I walk in Your way.
Open my ears to hear every word You will say.

Help me feel Your presence when I seek You,
Lead me to focus on Your will for all that I do.

Your love and approval is what I long to know,
And to honor You, Lord, because I love You so.

My plea is to always follow You in one accord,
I lift Your name up high as my Savior and Lord.

My whole life through, it's in You I put my trust,
With Heaven as our goal, faith in You we must.

August 18
LET ME BE AN INSTRUMENT

I will praise the LORD all my life;
I will sing praise to my God as long as I live.
Psalm 146:2 (NIV)

Lord, let me be an instrument to sing Your praises,
Let my words be a love song with joyous phrases.

I love You, Lord, with all my heart I come to pray.
You are my strength as I walk through every day.

You are the only One I trust, You make life whole,
Giving Your peace when burdens take their toll.

The happiness I share with You, no words can tell.
I'll praise You forever, for with my soul it is well.

Use my life, Lord, I humbly give it to Your hands.
Let me honor You according to Your divine plans.

August 19
MORE OF YOU AND LESS OF ME

"Ask, and it will be given to you; seek, and you will find;
knock, and it will be opened to you."
Matthew 7:7 (NKJV)

Lord, I want to glorify You with a humbled life.
Help me be thankful even through the strife.

I need more of You, Lord, and much less of me.
Provide a hunger each day for Your will to be.

Sitting in quietness, my mind is filled with You,
Lord, draw me closer as I trust You in all I do.

Let me be a difference in someone's life today,
Speak to me words to help them on their way.

Reveal Your beautiful presence so they can see.
Help them trust You to know salvation is free.

August 20
FOOD FOR MY SOUL

His divine power has given us everything required for life
and godliness through the knowledge of Him who called us
by His own glory and goodness.
2 Peter 1:3 (HCSB)

You are precious, Lord; I come before You now,
Whatever Your plans, with honor to You, I bow.

You are the morning sun that brings a new day,
And stars by night brightly lighting up my way.

You have provided everything we need to live,
And with grace our sins You came to forgive.

Your Spirit covers with overwhelming peace,
In Your strong arms, all worry begins to cease.

So many troubles of life attempt to take a toll,
Yet, Lord, Your mercy gives food for my soul.

On life's journey, You are always by my side.
Wherever You take me, You will be my guide.

August 21
MY REFUGE

In God is my salvation and my glory: the rock of my strength,
and my refuge, is in God.
Psalm 62:7 (KJV)

Lord, when I need more faith You are always here,
As my strength is weak, You remove all the fear.

When doubt creeps in, trying to hurt and destroy,
Your hand wipes away tears, restoring my joy.

When in the valley my concerns only You know,
I'll talk with You, Lord, because I trust You so.

When my soul's voice can't find the words to say,
I kneel in Your presence to listen and obey.

When life is full of distress and difficult to smile,
Lord, You are my refuge greater than any trial.

August 22
THE BEST GIFT

*For the wages of sin is death, but the free gift of God
is eternal life through Christ Jesus our Lord.
Romans 6:23 (NLT)*

You sent a beautiful butterfly to sit beside me today.
Lord, Your gift assured me my trials would be okay.

How quiet she sat as if to say, "I'm here just for you."
As I softly heard the words, "You'll see me through."

Gently she flew as delicate wings fluttered in the air,
The wonder of the moment revealed how You care.

I'm grateful how You made tiny creatures to be free,
While hearing all our prayers yet have time for me.

I'm no different from others, but You love me still,
For You know my heart longs to follow Your will.

Lord, I'm thankful for all gifts You abundantly give,
Yet Your best gift was given for everyone to live.

August 23
THROUGH OBEDIENCE

*"Therefore you shall love the LORD your God, and always
keep His charge, His statutes, His precepts, and His commandments,
it is your obligation to Him."*
Deuteronomy 11:1 (AMP)

God, thank You for creating this divine plan for me.
By sending Your precious Son so we can be set free.

You have designed the world, I'm just a small part.
Yet You see how I treasure You deep in my heart.

The depth of Your care I cannot ever understand,
I am so unworthy, but glad You have life planned.

Lord, by pleasing only You I want to finish strong,
Through obedience, You lead me as we walk along.

As my love deepens, earthly things seem to fade,
I'm thankful You came to save and sins You paid.

August 24
HOPE OF CHRIST

You will live secure and full of hope;
God will protect you and give you rest.
Job 11:18 (GNT)

I hear chatter of birds in the beauty You give,
It is a simple life, Lord, You allow them to live.

Their nests are built with creativity and flair,
For You give wisdom as they work with care.

They have no fear what tomorrow will bring,
In a beautiful chorus, they just happily sing.

Existing day to day, they really do not know.
How Your designs of nature will daily grow.

Lord, I will praise You for their words unsaid,
And for every blessing in this life and ahead.

They may not understand provision or trust,
Yet I'm glad the hope of Christ is true and just.

August 25
MY HEART SINGS, LORD

So my soul may sing praise to You, and not be quiet.
O Lord my God, I will give thanks to You forever.
Psalm 30:12 (NLV)

My heart sings, Lord, You've placed a song there,
Because of Your love, I'm blessed that You care.

Your goodness is abundant beyond any known,
Thank You for goodness You've always shown.

I am grateful for Your gift of divine, free grace.
And the promise of some day seeing Your face.

I'll walk the journey holding tight to Your hand,
And I will trust for whatever You have planned.

My heart sings, Lord, and Your name I will raise,
For You are worthy of all glory and all my praise.

August 26
Through the Wilderness

But Jesus beheld them, and said unto them, "With men this is impossible; but with God all things are possible."
Matthew 19:26 (KJV)

Lord, trials in life build walls only You can see through.
No matter how we try, there is nothing we can do.

The mighty power that You have shown from the grave,
Still lives today in You because You came here to save.

Your living water satisfies my soul, quenching my thirst,
I love You, Lord, in my heart You will always be first.

Without faith in You, Lord, there is nowhere else to cling,
All things are possible, You are truly Savior and King.

Thank You, Lord, through the wilderness You lead me,
When sight grows faint, Your Spirit helps me see.

August 27
STRENGTH FLOWS FROM YOUR THRONE

"Do not grieve, because the joy of the LORD is your strength."
Nehemiah 8:10 (CSB)

Heavenly Father, my heart is held in Your hand,
And no matter the trials with You, I will stand.

I long to be in Your presence with loving grace.
Alone in stillness, Lord, I pray to seek Your face.

There is a need God, that only Your hand can fill,
As You calm my anxious spirit, reveal Your will.

I thank You strength flows from Your throne.
And for joy and peace, more than I have known.

This journey is not easy, You said it wouldn't be.
In days as I struggle, I'm grateful You carry me.

August 28
LORD, HEAR MY HEART

*And we are sure of this, that he will listen to us whenever
we ask him for anything in line with his will.
1 John 5:14 (TLB)*

Lord, hear my heart as I pour out to You my prayer,
I'm thankful You go before me, my trials You bear.

Lord, help loved ones who really seek You today.
Healing is needed, please take care with no delay.

As Your truth grows deep to the depth of my soul,
I am strengthened, for our life is in Your control.

Allow me to enter Your divine presence as I pray.
Lord, lead us safely while we journey on our way.

As I spend time with You Your Spirit comforts me,
With every breath, I am glad I have been set free.

By faith Your light shines, restoring weary days,
As I seek You, Lord, Your name, I'll always praise.

August 29
BECAUSE OF YOUR GRACE

You, Lord, are forgiving and good,
abounding in love to all who call to you.
Psalm 86:5 (NIV)

Lord, Your name is exalted more than any on earth.
You are a perfect treasure greater than any worth.

In my memories I dwell on how precious You are,
There is none that compares, Lord, no one by far.

My soul is thirsty until I come before You in prayer,
You fill me up with Your steadfast love and care.

When covered by Your peace only then I can cope,
Thank You for mercy, You are my eternal hope.

For all the blessings, Lord, I will praise only You,
Because of Your grace, all souls are made new.

August 30
HEAVENLY BEAUTY

"For, behold, I create new heavens and a new earth;
and the former things shall not be remembered,
nor come into mind."
Isaiah 65:17 (ASV)

Lord, someday I'll be at home where I belong.
With You in eternity where nothing is wrong.

The day will come when I meet You in the air.
I'll never be alone for my loved ones are there.

We're here just moments until You come again,
When we seek forgiveness, You remove our sin.

No more worries for what will come tomorrow.
There will be no tears or painful earthly sorrow.

The angels will sing songs we have never heard,
Yet somehow our hearts will know every word.

All the earthly blessings we will never compare,
To the heavenly beauty, You are waiting to share.

August 31
WHILE I REST IN YOUR PRESENCE

Be on your guard; stand firm in the faith;
be courageous; be strong.
1 Corinthians 16:13 (NIV)

Lord, as I stand in Your presence, what will You say?
I try to imagine Your face as I humbly bow that day.

I think about the Cross, why You came here to save,
And how grateful I am, You rose from the grave.

There are those who follow You throughout their life,
They always honor You while struggling in strife.

Yet there are some who dwell on what this life brings,
Their satisfaction lies in desiring all earthly things.

Lord, help me be obedient, I give You humble praise.
I will seek in following in all Your wonderful ways.

I'll stand strong in burdens as long as You are here,
Without You, life would hold emptiness and fear.

Thank You for guiding me, my desire is in Your will,
While I rest in Your presence, Lord, I will be still.

September

September 1
WHEN HOPE BEGINS TO FADE

He restores my soul. He leads me in paths
of righteousness for his name's sake.
Psalm 23:3 (RSV)

Lord, as long as I have You, I have everything.
You put joy in my soul, making my heart sing.

It is Your light that rises in me each new day,
And it gives me strength to travel on my way.

Joy makes me smile as I think of Your name.
I'm grateful, Lord, You always stay the same.

You renew my faith when hope begins to fade,
You took my sins and with Your life You paid.

Your Word says to trust in Your divine plans,
I am so thankful my life is held in Your hands.

September 2
I Need to Hear from You, God

And he said to them, "Pay attention to what you hear:
with the measure you use, it will be measured to you,
and still more will be added to you."
Mark 4:24 (ESV)

God, please comfort me through this trial today.
I will patiently wait for what it is You have to say.

As I pray for Your plan and guidance for Your will,
I need to hear from You, God, while I remain still.

In listening to birds singing and buzzing of the bees,
I feel Your peacefulness flowing through the trees.

You're visible in the cool water, rippled by the wind,
Your beauty is shown from day's sunrise until end.

When I think of how You gave and battles You won,
I'm humbled by Your mercy given through Your Son.

My heart is so grateful because You gave Your best,
I will stay in Your presence, it is with You I find rest.

September 3
I WILL NOT WALK IN DEFEAT

*But the Lord is faithful, and He will strengthen you
[setting you on a firm foundation] and will protect
and guard You from the evil one.*
2 Thessalonians 3:3 (AMP)

Lord, I search my heart to express words to You,
For You have known my love is devoted and true.

At sunrise I long to meet You in morning prayer,
Somehow I just know You will be with me there.

Through storms You cover me with gentle peace,
As You call out burdens telling them to cease.

You are my warrior in the giant battles You fight,
I thank You, Lord, for Your strength and might.

I will not walk in defeat for failure holds no hope,
Only with You, Lord, I know I can always cope.

I am so grateful, Your love and grace are mine,
For today, tomorrow and through endless time.

September 4
THROUGH EVERY VALLEY

Let this same attitude and purpose and [humble]
mind be in you which was in Christ Jesus:
[Let Him be your example in humility:]
Philippians 2:5 (AMPC)

Lord, when I think of grace Your Word rings true,
And in my heart Your strength carries me through.

There is safety in Your arms where I want to stay.
As I come to You seeking peace as I kneel to pray.

I'll lean on Your promises You've divinely planned.
For You have given wisdom to help me understand.

Teach me, Lord, to be humble waiting in Your time,
Through every valley I walk and mountain I climb.

Please hear words of praise as I offer them to You,
Your goodness, Lord, has blessed me in all You do.

September 5
FORGIVENESS IS ENDLESS

*"I, I am he who blots out your transgressions
for my own sake, and I will not remember your sins."
Isaiah 43:25 (ESV)*

Lord, when I come to You all my troubles cease,
In those moments, I'm filled with joy and peace.

Thank You for Your grace lovingly given to me.
Your promises are many I'll always thank Thee.

When my mind wanders I'm drawn back to You,
By Your Holy Spirit, always leading me through.

Pleasing You is always the desire of my heart,
As thankfulness overflows and fills every part.

Lord, I am grateful for Your mercy when I fail,
Your forgiveness is endless, You always prevail.

September 6
OPEN THEIR HEARTS, LORD

I will give them one heart [a new heart], and put a new spirit within them. I will take from them the heart of stone, and will give them a heart of flesh [that is responsive to My touch].
Ezekiel 11:19 (AMP)

Lord, let the fire of Your Spirit burn through me.
Let my heart reflect Your love for others to see.

Grow in me the peace that flows from Your heart,
With roots deep in my soul, intertwine each part.

Speak to me, Lord, when someone is led astray,
Teach me as I pray in finding right words to say.

Show them Your truth as they seek Your Word.
Open their hearts, Lord, to all they have heard.

Allow me to share Your truth in the right ways,
And to stay close to You all the rest of my days.

September 7
In Your Presence

My heart says of you, "Seek his face!"
Your face, LORD, I will seek.
Psalm 27:8 (NIV)

Lord, how do I thank You for Your divine love?
How do I express my thoughts to You above?

Every moment I will honor You all of my days,
With love, be pleased with my humble praise.

When in Your presence pouring out my heart,
You bring me close for nothing takes us apart.

Lord, let my ears be open to hear Your voice,
Help me discern in making the right choice.

Allow, my words to glorify You in every way.
As I soak in Your beauty on this amazing day.

September 8
EVERY DAY CLOSER

Do not worry about tomorrow. Tomorrow will have it's own worries.
The troubles we have in a day are enough for one day.
Matthew 6:34 (NLV)

Father, place in my heart a new praise song each day.
Help me dwell on Your will as I quietly kneel to pray.

Give me faith that conquers all earthly doubt and fear,
Please speak to me, Holy Spirit, because I need to hear.

Your comfort is real each time I come to cry or rejoice,
Every day, Lord, I seek while listening for Your voice.

In cold and dark nights, Your peace keeps me warm,
While strength brings calm to the frightening storm.

Lord, You have given me many blessings, this is true,
I'm thankful for Your grace every day closer to You.

September 9
DIVINE TREASURE OF WORTH

And He will be the security and stability of your times,
A treasure of salvation, wisdom and knowledge;
The fear of the LORD is your treasure.
Isaiah 33:6 (AMP)

Lord, I really do need and love You more each day.
I long to hear Your voice as I journey upon my way.

Your goodness creates in my heart a happy love song,
Because to You, Lord, I will always faithfully belong.

I see Your presence in the rising of the morning sun,
And I know whatever happens with You I have won.

Thank You for grace You've abundantly shown to me.
Through battles, my eyes have been opened to see.

Your Word is awesome, a divine treasure of worth.
Filled with Your wisdom, nothing is greater on earth.

I praise You for peace because of You I have found,
My heavenly foundation, I'll stand on solid ground.

September 10
GRACE GREATER

But you, Lord, are a compassionate and gracious God,
slow to anger and abounding in faithful love and truth.
Psalm 86:15 (CSB)

Father, hear my heart's praise to You today,
As I speak be blessed by these words I say.

Lord, let my life magnify You every day long,
For You've written in my soul a joyful song.

You are Master and King over all the earth,
Thank You for hope through Your holy birth.

As I enter the valley and on to the mountain,
Your strength is the only sustaining fountain.

I will glorify Your name, Lord, forevermore,
For grace greater than sand on every shore.

September 11
EVERY TIME, LORD

*No temptation has overtaken you except what is common to mankind. And
God is faithful; he will not let you be tempted beyond what you can bear.
But when you are tempted, he will also provide a way out so that you can
endure it.*
1 Corinthians 10:13 (NIV)

Lord, every time I've been down, You lifted me up.
Every time I feel empty, You always fill my cup.

Lord, every time I'm in need, You always provide,
Every time my heart is broken, in You I can hide.

Lord, every time there's doubt, You show me trust,
Every time I am uncertain, Your outcome is just.

Lord, every time I'm lonely, You are here with me.
Every time I want my will, let it be Yours I see.

Lord, every time I'm wrong, by grace You forgive,
Every time I fail, I'm reminded in You I still live.

Lord, every time I praise, it's because You I love,
Every time I pray, I'll always honor You above.

September 12
SOMETIMES THERE IS A TEST

But He knows the way that I take;
When He has tested me, I shall come forth as gold.
Job 23:10 (NKJV)

Lord, help me feel Your presence and to obey.
Please don't let my will find reason for delay.

As You lead me through this journey in life,
I ask Your favor to endure the earthly strife.

Whenever burdens become such a heavy load,
Lord, keep me from leaving the destined road.

Sometimes before You answer there is a test,
Yet while in the valley it is there I find rest.

Lord, grant wisdom in what You ask me to do.
Please give me strength in following through.

You are my Savior whom I will always love,
And my divine gift sent from Heaven above.

September 13
There Is a Purpose

I cry out to God Most High,
to God who will fulfill his purpose for me.
Psalm 57:2 (NLT)

Lord, some prayers You answer, others You deny,
Yet, I will not question or wonder the reason why.

Your peace is with me even when my faith is weak,
For in trials it is Your strength I will forever seek.

Lord, Your presence is always boundless and real,
How You removed hurt that never seemed to heal.

I'm thankful, Lord, for Your steadfast divine hope,
And all the times I've needed Your Spirit to cope.

There is a purpose for all things You have allowed,
Let my heart be faithful, humble and never proud.

September 14
REJOICE IN MY WORSHIP

Let the heavens be glad and let the earth rejoice;
and let men say among the nations, "The Lord reigns!"
1 Chronicles 16:31 (AMPC)

Lord, my cup is filled with You, I desire even more.
I will stand on Your Word, because it is You I adore.

Our life is here today with no guarantee tomorrow,
Yet You came to restore hearts, broken by sorrow.

Lord, it is Your Spirit's guidance we always need,
Please humble my heart, saving from sin's greed.

I am thankful for direction, with You I rise above,
Life is a blessing because of Your sacrificial love.

Rejoice in my worship You're worthy and praised,
As I lift my eyes toward Heaven with hands raised.

September 15
WHO AM I, LORD?

Delight yourself in the LORD,
and he will give you the desires of your heart.
Psalm 37:4 (NASB)

Who Am I, Lord, to be blessed by the goodness of You?
I am unworthy, yet in the valleys You lead me through.

Who am I, Lord, unworthy of Your precious life You gave?
I am undeserving, but You still came to earth to save.

Who Am I, Lord, to have a priceless friend as Thee?
I am so humbled, You sacrificed Your life for lowly me.

Who Am I, Lord, to be comforted by Your peaceful love?
I am so grateful, for Your everlasting arms from above.

Who Am I, Lord, to be assured You hear every prayer?
I am so thankful, because of Your tenderness and care.

Who Am I, Lord, to hear Your gentle Spirit quietly speak?
I am overjoyed, for You are the One I will forever seek.

September 16
WHILE I LEARN TO BE STILL

You need endurance, so that after you have done God's will,
you may receive what was promised.
Hebrews 10:36 (HCSB)

Good Morning God, I awoke thankful for Your Son,
Great joy overwhelms my soul for all He has done.

Your hope is present in the breath of each new day,
You walk with me through the valleys along my way.

Allow me to know the desires of Your planned will.
And please help me endure while I learn to be still.

You draw my heart closer, always devoted to You,
And my soul rejoices because of everything You do.

Your presence is sweet as the fragrance of the rose,
Your strength is powerful more than anyone knows.

Lord, as I travel this journey, I'm thankful for grace.
And the promise of Heaven, a most beautiful place.

September 17
LET ME MAKE A DIFFERENCE

And whatever you do, whether in word or deed,
do it all in the name of the Lord Jesus,
giving thanks to God the Father through him.
Colossians 3:17 (NIV)

Draw me close, Lord, I will trust You in all I do,
As I sit in stillness, my mind is filled with You.

Teach me how to be content with a humbled life,
Let my heart be thankful as I live through strife.

Give me a hunger for Your presence so I can see.
I will always desire more of You and less of me.

In life there are those that need to turn from sin,
Lord, open doors for hurting hearts to let You in.

Let me make a difference in someone's life today,
Speak to me, my Lord, to help them on their way.

Allow Your Holy Spirit to shine brightly through.
To encourage others in placing their trust in You.

September 18
BATTLES IN YOUR TIMING

He stores up sound wisdom for the upright;
he is a shield to those who walk in integrity.
Proverbs 2:7 (RSV)

Father, You are the maker of all Heaven and earth,
You turn night to morning as the sun gives birth.

I am so grateful for Your bountiful blessings to me,
Through Your eyes in trials, You allowed me to see.

In walking through the valleys You faithfully guide,
I will give honor and glory as You walk by my side.

You are a priceless treasure, much higher than gold.
My life rests in Your hands, I trust You always hold.

I'm truly humbled, Lord, I come joyfully in prayer.
Battles in Your timing are victories for us to share.

September 19
NO GREATER MOMENTS

For God alone my soul waits in silence and quietly
submits to Him, For my hope is from Him.
Psalm 62:5 (AMP)

Lord, I come quietly into Your presence today,
While sun shines in my heart, yet skies are gray.

As moments pass Your peace makes joy anew,
In my safe place, where time is spent with You.

There is abundant hope for all my tomorrows,
And Your mercy restores by removing sorrows.

You alone are more wonderful than I can say,
I long to be with You, Lord, as I listen and pray.

No greater moments than those in Your care,
As Your Word speaks to me I find rest there.

September 20
THROUGH TESTING

The tested genuineness of your faith ... may be found to result in praise and glory and honor at the revelation of Jesus Christ.
1 Peter 1:7 (ESV)

Lord, there isn't always happiness walking by sight.
It's the journey in darkness when we see Your light.

As we go through trials abundant mercy will flow,
Pain is for a season in the appointed time, You know.

It is easy to trust when on the mountain we stand,
But in the valleys You draw closer, holding our hand.

Through testing we're stretched to grow in strength,
As we patiently wait no matter how long the length.

Lord, I will be grateful for blessings forever more.
Wherever You may lead and whatever is in store.

September 21
ALL HEAVEN SINGS

Lord, let my praise be a sweet sound in Your ears,
And Your soft whisper be all my heart ever hears.

As I kneel in Your presence, it is on holy ground,
Because You are Lord, Your glory there is found.

Through all my days and into every silent night,
You comfort me in the stillness of the moonlight.

To speak of Your grace, the humbleness is mine,
As Your name is magnified Your light will shine.

To love You is most treasured above all things.
As I praise You, Lord, I imagine all Heaven sings.

September 22
TEACH ME TO WAIT

"Teaching them to observe all that I have commanded you.
And behold, I am with you always, to the end of the age."
Matthew 28:20 (ESV)

Help me, sweet Spirit, to walk the journey today.
Speak words of wisdom through whatever I say.

Fill my heart with Your grace and abundant love,
Give me a thirst to seek humbleness from above.

Let me have peace as I live in Your divine will,
Show me understanding when I climb every hill.

Draw me with Your whisper as You speak to me,
I truly need Your guidance, Lord, this You see.

Teach me to wait, being patience through delay,
Holy Spirit, I'm glad You are with me every day.

September 23
THROUGH SAVING GRACE

The LORD is merciful and gracious,
slow to anger and abounding in steadfast love.
Psalm 103:8 (RSV)

God, it is amazing to know You created everything.
How You made the sun to shine and birds to sing.

Daily I see the beauty and thankful for every hour,
As Your nature comes alive birthing each flower.

The sky and water You made are wonderfully vast,
I trust in the assurance Your love will always last.

I look for You in the break of every brilliant day,
Oh, how I long to be with You walking on my way.

You formed the world with mastery and great flair,
I thank You, Lord, because You hear every prayer.

My heart is grateful for all You have done for me,
Through saving grace, You opened my eyes to see.

September 24
A Humble Vessel

"If anyone serves me, he must follow me; and where I am,
there will my servant be also. If anyone serves me,
the Father will honor him."
John 12:26 (ESV)

Dear Lord, guide me in all Your wonderful ways.
Help me to hear Your voice the rest of my days.

Thoughts of You fill my mind when I am alone.
As Your grace flows from Your heavenly throne.

My hope is to be molded by Your loving hands.
To be a humble vessel used in Your divine plans.

While I travel the journey, my heart is with You,
Each step is strengthened, making my path new.

There's joy following the promise of Your Word.
As peace fills my soul, Your whispers are heard.

Lord, I'm thankful Your Holy Spirit lives within.
Please reveal Your ways as I rise daily to begin.

September 25
FAITH IS NOT IN VAIN

So then faith comes by hearing, and hearing
by the word of God.
Romans 10:17 (NKJV)

Lord, let Your heart be touched by humble praise.
As I come into Your presence joyful for Thy ways.

You are so faithful, yet it is for nothing I have done,
My trust rests in You, Lord, for You are God's Son.

In devoted prayer, I draw closer to You each day,
Even when the journey seems so cloudy and gray.

Thank You for peace, I know my faith is not in vain,
For I trust in You through trouble and all the pain.

Life is so uncertain trying to understand Your will,
Yet You see our empty hearts and You come to fill.

September 26
I Praise You for Blessings

*Praise the God and Father of our Lord Jesus Christ, who has
blessed us in Christ with every spiritual blessing in the heavens.
Ephesians 1:3 (HCSB)*

Dear Lord, I need to feel Your presence today.
Help my thoughts stay focused and not to sway.

Sometimes the trials weigh heavy on my mind,
But I'm grateful I have You, so loving and kind.

You are with me in the storms and bright days.
I love You, Lord, trusting You in all Your ways.

My steps are destined and guided by Your hand,
No one can change what You divinely planned.

You know of our past and the end has been set.
Through the grace You gave, You paid our debt.

Lord, I praise You for all blessings You bestow,
For I am Your child and I know You love me so.

September 27
I Take Refuge in You

*Every word of God proves true; he is a shield
to those who take refuge in him.
Proverbs 30:5 (ESV)*

Heavenly Father, what would we do without You?
There would be no strength to carry through.

Life would hold no hope or Your promise to give,
With long days so difficult without You to live.

Some cry in anguish, yet some ask reasons why,
As others look for signs written in the sky.

Certain times You have said, "Be patient and wait,"
Your answers will come and never too late.

I'm thankful You promise to be with us each day,
While I bow on my knees, faithfully to pray.

I need You, Lord Jesus, I take refuge in You alone.
And one day I'll see You upon Your throne.

September 28
FAITH IS NEVER AMISS

I have chosen the way of faithfulness;
I have set my heart on your laws.
Psalm 119:30 (NIV)

Lord, when we trust not in ourselves but in You,
We don't have to worry for You see us through.

Your love breaks every chain that binds us tight,
For our lives change, when guided by Your sight.

In weakness, the enemy tries to steal peace away,
But strength arises in Your presence as we pray.

Lord, Your healing comes in brokenness or tears.
For You are always with us to erase all our fears.

With You we have the divine power to prevail,
Because of Your sweet grace whenever we fail.

Lord, life built on You is filled with eternal bliss,
When hearts are humbled, faith is never amiss.

September 29
UNFAILING LOVE

You are a hiding place; You keep me from trouble;
You surround me with songs of deliverance.
Psalm 32:7 (NASB)

Lord, in my quiet place I praise Your name.
It is there I kneel daily where peace I claim.

Above all, it is only You I truly seek and adore,
In every season, I've learned I need You more.

On winding paths, I am guided always by You,
For Your Spirit is faithful to lead me through,

There is no better companion or greater friend,
With You it is precious time I want to spend.

Lord, in trials I cry out and You meet me there,
Your unfailing love is given with divine care.

September 30
WHEN LIFE TRIALS ARE WEARY

For the eyes of the Lord search back and forth across the whole earth, looking for people whose hearts are perfect toward him, so that he can show his great power in helping them ...
2 Chronicles 16:9 (TLB)

Lord, I need Your Spirit to guide me on the way.
You are the Good Shepherd I will trust and obey.

Thank You, Lord, for Your forgiveness when I fail,
And for Your amazing grace when my faith is frail.

When life trials are weary, You are always there,
It is You I seek while burdens are difficult to bear.

I will forever praise You, Lord, through the end.
You are my Comforter and most treasured friend.

All I have to give is my devoted praise and love,
Lord, let my worship flow to Your heart above.

October

October 1

DARKNESS HAS NO HOLD

He Himself bore our sins in his body on the tree;
so that, having died to sins, we might live for righteousness.
By his wounds you have been healed.
I Peter 2:24 (CSB)

Dear Lord, I have little to offer but just a prayer,
Yet You see how much I love You and how I care.

As I think of the Cross and where You have been,
I am reminded of the burdens with chains of sin.

When I dwell on how You suffered, bled and died,
How they treated You and when You were tried.

You knew the pain Your body would go through,
For our eternal life, rests on trusting in only You.

It saddens my heart, for it's our guilt You bore.
But I'm grateful darkness has no hold any more.

Lord, if it wasn't for Your grace You freely give,
I wouldn't have Your hope and strength to live.

October 2
AS WE WALK TOGETHER

For we are his workmanship, created in Christ Jesus for good works,
which God prepared beforehand, that we should walk in them.
Ephesians 2:10 (RSV)

Lord, I can't see tomorrow yet I trust in You,
While I think of trials You've led me through.

As I look back Your abundant blessings I see,
I'm thankful You faithfully watched over me.

Lord, guide my path with steps I am to take.
I give all to You the decisions I must make.

I won't submit to fear in facing the unknown,
Because I believe I'll never be left all alone.

Let me hear Your voice as we walk together.
With You by my side any test I can weather.

October 3
Joy That Fills My Soul

Because of this, we are made right with God by His loving-favor.
Now we can have life that lasts forever as He has promised.
Titus 3:7 (NLV)

Lord, I am glad You hold my life in Your hands.
And grateful to follow a path led by Your plans.

As I dwell on Your love and the depth You care,
Your presence restores like a breath of fresh air.

Your strength instructs mountains to stand tall,
Yet this earth will end someday upon Your call.

As I trust in Your sovereignty and divine grace,
I cherish the promise one day to see Your face.

Lord, You're the peace and joy that fills my soul,
Because of You, I am forgiven and made whole.

October 4
THE ONE WHO GAVE

*"For even I, the Messiah, am not here to be served, but
to help others, and to give my life as a ransom for many."*
Mark 10:45 (TLB)

Lord, in this quiet time You make my worries cease.
As the joy flows from Heaven, I receive Your peace.

There is sweet comfort in hours I spend with You,
I just need to hold Your hand as I walk through.

Life's purpose would be void if You were not here,
Without You, Lord, my days would be lived in fear.

The earthly trials somehow try to pull me away,
Yet You have my heart every moment of the day.

You're the One who gave Your perfect life for me.
Through Your shed blood, I am eternally set free.

Thank You, Jesus, for all that You faithfully give.
Because of Your sacrifice, now I will forever live.

October 5
ON THE CROSS

But the scripture says that the whole world is under the power
of sin; and so the gift which is promised on the basis of faith
in Jesus Christ is given to those who believe.
Galatians 3:22 (GNT)

Lord, on the Cross You died in our place.
You bore our sin fulfilled by Your grace.

It is there where our wounds are healed,
And You became our Savior and shield.

You came to restore the sick and the lame,
As many suffer from sadness and shame.

Lord, You sacrificed to bring eternal life,
While You carried our ugly sin and strife.

On the Cross You saw weakness and pain,
It was our life held by the enemy's chain.

Lord, because of Your gift we live again.
And no longer are bound by worldly sin.

October 6
PRAISE THROUGH TEARS

So my soul may sing praise to You, and not be quiet.
O Lord my God, I will give thanks to You forever.
Psalm 30:12 (NLV)

Lord, I long to talk to You every morning as I rise,
And say good night each evening as I close my eyes.

For Your blessings I'll thank You every time I pray,
Even through the testing You send amid my day.

Often I am awakened with many thoughts of You,
Yet Your presence gives rest all the night through.

You are wonderful, Lord, for goodness You show,
And for Your peace and joy, I have grown to know.

I'll honor You for Your true love and divine grace.
As You hear my praise through tears on my face.

Thank You for loving enough to give up life for me,
It is through Your sacrifice my heart can truly see.

October 7
PROTECTION THROUGH TRIALS

Whoever listens to me will live in safety
and be at ease, without fear of harm."
Proverbs 1:33 (NIV)

Lord, I will honor You each moment of the day.
To praise and glorify You every step of the way.

Your grace has given me far more than I deserve,
Let me honor You by opening my heart to serve.

Some days my mind is weary and body is weak,
I need to be with You to hear Your Spirit speak.

I am unworthy, yet I know I'm led by Your light.
For Your Word says, I am precious in Your sight.

Thank You, Lord, for Your mercy granted to me.
And Your protection through trials I don't see.

October 8
LORD JESUS, BE BLESSED

"For I will proclaim the name [and Presence] of the LORD;
ascribe greatness and honor to our God!"
Deuteronomy 32:3 (AMP)

Lord, teach me how to honor You and how to forgive.
I want to glorify Your name every moment I live.

Show me how to see truth from Your matchless Word.
Let me share You from what my heart has heard.

Lord, give me a spirit of boldness to magnify only You.
Help me love through Your eyes, as You always do.

Please strengthen when I stumble for my body is weak,
As days are weary, You are the only One I seek.

Lord Jesus, be blessed with my humble praises today.
I surrender to Your Spirit to guide each word I say.

October 9
SWEET MEMORIES OF MY DAY

May my meditation be pleasing to him;
I will rejoice in the LORD.
Psalm 104:34 (CSB)

Lord, thank You for the love and peace You give,
Your goodness is displayed in this world we live.

I sit by the peaceful stream as water runs cold,
With my thoughts of You, I feel time is on hold.

As the sunsets reveal the quiet moonlit nights,
The darkness awakes with soft twinkling lights.

I love to praise You, Lord, through the day long.
Joy is in my soul where You have placed a song.

I cherish meditating in Your presence as I pray,
For these times are sweet memories of my day.

October 10
You Can Do What I Can't

"Submit to God and be at peace with him; ... Accept instruction from his mouth and lay up his words in your heart.
Job 22:21-22 (NIV)

Lord, is it right to ask You for reasons why?
When our lives are shattered and hearts cry.

I know we are to trust and patiently be still,
Yet some days it's hard to wait on Your will.

Lord, I'm just human as You have created me.
Please help me with wisdom and eyes to see.

With mercy my prayers You faithfully grant,
And Lord, I believe You can do what I can't.

Thank You for listening to my every request,
I praise You, Lord, for in Your presence I rest.

October 11
PRECIOUS ARMS OF LOVE

The LORD appeared to us in the past, saying:
"I have loved you with an everlasting love;
I have drawn you with unfailing kindness."
Jeremiah 31:3 (NIV)

Lord, You hold my heart in Your gentle way,
As I seek Your peace in the words, You say.

What can I do, Lord, to honor You even more?
You know I trust whatever You have in store.

Through eternity souls remain in Your hands,
And Lord, I'll continue to wait on Your plans.

In sadness I've cried and You're always there,
With Joy, I have rejoiced for I know you care.

Thank You, Father, as You reign from above.
And for extending Your precious arms of love.

October 12
MY CHILD BE STRONG

*Withhold not Your tender mercy from me, O Lord; let Your
loving-kindness and Your truth continually preserve me!
Psalm 40:11 (AMPC)*

Lord, I have an image of You walking with me.
We are in the valley but the path I can't see.

In dark days Your arms will carry me along,
As You softly whisper, "My child be strong."

I feel no worry there because I can trust You,
My soul is at peace for You help me through.

If I cry You wipe away dread and every tear,
As You tell me there is no reason for my fear.

Yet Lord, I'll need Your strength as I get weak,
But You can see, You are the only One I seek.

Lord, I'm Yours and You will forever be mine,
As I walk joyfully with You throughout time.

October 13
A Glorious Day

The signs of Your return, Lord, are drawing near,
Because I trust You, I will have no reason to fear.

It will be a glorious day when we see Your face,
When we finally are taken to our heavenly place.

You will come with power in the blink of an eye,
Many will be happy, yet other ones will only cry.

When You arrive Your mighty call will be heard,
Some will leave quickly, according to Your Word.

All those who have passed have all become new,
And everyone who is alive will witness that too.

We all will praise with hands raised to the sky,
Giving thanks to our God on His throne up high.

Until then, Lord, we will wait believing in You,
While trusting Your arms to carry us through.

October 14
WHEN WE SURRENDER

"Not everyone who says to Me, 'Lord, Lord,'
will enter the kingdom of heaven, but only he
who does the will of My Father who is in heaven."
Matthew 7:21 (AMP)

Lord, Your awesome beauty pleases my eyes,
As the clouds pass through boundless skies.

I ponder how You created great and small,
With glorious streams and mountains tall.

This world was made by Your mighty hand,
And in Your presence someday I will stand.

I wonder why many cannot see their wrong?
Yet in Your loving grace, You carry us along.

When we surrender accepting Your Spirit in,
Your love and mercy gives freedom from sin.

You have granted blessings beyond compare,
I'll praise You as I kneel humbled in prayer.

October 15
SEEDS OF LOVE

"You shall therefore love the LORD your God
and keep his charge, his statutes, his ordinances,
and his commandments always."
Deuteronomy 11:1 (RSV)

Lord, You've planted in my soul seeds of love,
As I follow in Your ways from Heaven above.

Knowing You love me springs up joy within,
As I rise each morning to praise You again.

I'll thank You, Father, even if all goes wrong.
And whenever the roads seem way too long.

In sunshine and darkness I will look to You,
Because I know, Lord, You'll see me through.

Please fill my life with Your presence Lord,
Let our hearts be intertwined in one accord.

I will always rejoice because I need You so,
To worship You, Lord, helps my faith grow.

October 16
MORE THAN ENOUGH

*His divine power has granted to us all things that
pertain to life and godliness, through the knowledge
of him who called us to his own glory and excellence.*
2 Peter 1:3 (ESV)

Thank You, Lord, for the air I breathe each day.
And for Your provisions as I journey on my way.

Your blessings are showered like rain from above,
There is no greater gift than Your abundant love.

You always know my need even in clouds of doubt,
Providing more than enough before time runs out.

I'm grateful for Your Spirit, who gives such peace.
You help me see through Your eyes as trials cease.

My heart is not chained to any earthly treasure,
It's only Your presence that brings such pleasure.

October 17
ALL THINGS ARE BLESSINGS

The LORD is good to all,
and his mercy is over all that he has made.
Psalm 145:9 (ESV)

Lord, there is no end to Your goodness and love,
As that of the rainbow, You lovingly set above.

I hear Your voice in the special ways You speak,
As I spend time in prayer, it is only You I seek.

It's wondrous how the moon sits perfectly still,
Yet mighty storms can rage guided at Your will.

You are awesome, Lord; I am so amazed by You,
How all things are blessings through all You do.

I thank You, Lord, for Your abundance of grace.
As I bow before You, each day in this quiet place.

October 18
It's All in Your Time

But as for me, I trust in You, O LORD;
I say, "You are my God."
Psalm 31:14 (NKJV)

Lord, I know Your steadfast love is ever so true.
With each breath I take, I'll humbly praise You.

You see my thoughts and You hear every plea,
I only wish I could give You more than just me.

As we walk together through the darkest days,
I'll trust even if not understanding Your ways.

In valleys and mountains, I struggle to climb.
With faith in You, I know it's all in Your time.

I thank You for joy because in You I can rest,
And I praise You, Lord, for I'm truly blessed.

October 19
LORD, USE ME

*"Let your light so shine before men, that they may see
your good works, and glorify your Father which is in heaven."
Matthew 5:16 (KJV)*

Lord, give me tender words from Your heart to say,
Please cross my path with those needing help today.

Let me reach them if they have not trusted in You,
I pray You will give them peace to make it through.

Lord, use me to reflect Your goodness and true love,
To tell others why You came from Your home above.

You hear my cry whenever I come to You in prayer.
For You are here catching every single tear I bear.

Help me to never fail in bringing Your name glory,
Give me favor, Lord, in telling of Your divine story.

October 20
Grace Changes Lives

*For sin shall not be master over you, for
you are not under the law but under grace.
Romans 6:14 (NASB)*

Lord, it is beautiful how You created birds to sing,
And butterflies adorned with their delicate wings.

You thought of everything to make our world good,
It must sadden You why some haven't understood.

You came to remove all our sin and earthly strife,
As we give our hearts to You receiving eternal life.

Lord, Your goodness is revealed through each day,
While Your Word teaches things, we need to obey.

Let Your voice be heard by whispers in our ears.
As grace changes lives, wiping away all the tears.

October 21

The Mountain Seems So High

But let him ask in faith without doubting. For the doubter
is like the surging sea, driven and tossed by the wind.
James 1:6 (HCSB)

Lord, draw me near for I really need You now,
To get through this journey, I'm not sure how.

In this hard time, I seek Your strength to cope,
Please fill my heart with Your peace and hope.

The way is safe walking with You hand in hand,
I will not doubt but wait for what You planned.

From my view, Lord, mountains seem so high.
But as I walk in this valley, I will not ask why.

My faith rests in You and I will remain strong,
As I set my eyes on You, Lord, every day long.

In this moment I lay all my trials at Your feet,
For I know my needs You are faithful to meet.

October 22

In Thankfulness Each Day

Serve the LORD with gladness!
Come into his presence with singing!
Psalm 100:2 (ESV)

Lord, how precious is Your divine love to me,
Draw me near, Lord, even closer to Thee.

I will praise You, for I know Your Spirit is here,
And for peace You grant in hours of fear.

Your eyes see what I need before I arrive there.
You always give freely because You care.

Your gentle mercy makes my humble heart sing,
Lord, it is to Your hand I will forever cling.

I lose myself in thankfulness for You each day,
When I seek You, Lord, as I come to pray.

October 23
YOU WILL MAKE A WAY

I am your God and will take care of you ... I made you
and will care for you; I will give you help and rescue you.
Isaiah 46:4 (GNT)

Precious Lord, I long to meet You again today,
Please accept my praise and worship as I pray.

You know my heart and answers we all need,
Help me know Your will, I'm asking You to lead.

Without Your presence, how would I ever live?
Lord, I'm humbled because You came to forgive.

My sadness became joy the moment I met You,
In those weary days, You brought me through.

Your beauty is more abundant than any I see,
And Your love more gracious than any can be.

I pour out prayer and praises to You this day,
For I know in my heart You will make a way.

October 24
At Your Feet

Give thanks to the Lord, for He is good;
His faithful love endures forever!
1 Chronicles 16:34 (HCSB)

Lord, my safe place is found in Your love.
There I find hope given to me from above.

You walk with me daily guiding my way,
And You mold like a potter shaping clay.

My faith rests in You every breath I take,
With my trust in You, each step I make.

Through trials as I kneel quietly to pray,
Your presence sustains in night and day.

Our forgiveness is free, sacrificed by You,
For You have been hurt and felt pain too.

At Your feet, I praise for all You have done,
With you, the battles are not lost but won.

October 25
BURDEN MY HEART

---

*"For it is not you who are speaking, but the Spirit
of your Father speaking through you."*
Matthew 10:20 (AMPC)

Lord, I have pondered, how can I glorify You?
Allow me to see through Your eyes in all I do.

In quiet prayer, I cry for those saddened faces.
As I see hopelessness with tear stained traces.

Help them, for they may not know Your grace.
And Lord, open blinded eyes to seek Your face.

I want to be a witness, please burden my heart,
Show me Your true desire and I'll do my part.

Lord, I pray for troubles they've been through.
Somehow let me tell them to trust only in You.

October 26
The Only Hope

Teach me, O Lord, the way of Your statutes;
and I will keep it to the end.
Psalm 119:33 (AMPC)

Lord, You are the only hope for eternity ahead,
When valleys feel hopeless and hard to tread.

Your peace brings comfort in days and night,
As I bow in prayer, divine mercy reveals sight.

Your eyes see my heart, I truly need You here.
Lord, thank You for drawing me ever so near.

I seek to know Your will, teach me Your ways,
As I follow You, Lord, all the rest of my days.

I love Your Word, for Your promises are true.
I'll stay close to You while we walk through.

October 27
LORD, YOU ARE ABLE

Now to him who is able to do far more abundantly
than all that we ask or think, according to the
power at work within us.
Ephesians 3:20 (ESV)

In Your will, Lord, souls can calmly rest.
As You hold us near, we're truly blessed.

You are able to do all things we can't do,
While we trust and give our trials to You.

There is no pain Your love cannot heal,
No matter the problem or how we feel.

I'm so thankful eternity is in Your plans,
As You keep our life in Your holy hands.

Lord, my praise and honor I give today.
I'll place at the altar as I kneel to pray.

October 28
If I Looked in Your Eyes, Lord

For God's eyes are on the ways of a man, and He sees all his steps.
Job 34:21 (AMP)

Lord, as I travel this journey, a life given to me,
I'll trust in only You for what my path shall be.

My heart is grateful for Your goodness and love,
And the abundance of grace given from above.

If I looked in Your eyes, Lord, what would I find?
Are there tears from our burdens on Your mind?

Or would I see joy in Your heart that overflows?
For only You have answers no one else knows.

Lord, let my life honor in all You want me to do.
While Your Holy Spirit guides every day anew.

October 29
ACTS OF LOVE

I have no greater joy than to hear that my children walk in truth.
3 John 1:4 (KJV)

With every breath, Lord, Your goodness I will proclaim,
I walk each day in gratitude to praise Your Holy Name.

You are my Father, greater than any treasure on earth.
Lord, nothing compares in depth to Your divine worth.

Your Holy Spirit is with me each morning when I rise,
Your awesome beauty surrounds me as I lift my eyes.

God, thank You for abundance You have provided me,
I am grateful You always hear my heart's every plea.

All Your wonderful ways have blessed in acts of love,
As You watch and gently guide from Heaven above.

October 30
LORD, HOW DO I THANK YOU?

Enter into his gates with thanksgiving,
And into his courts with praise:
Be thankful unto him, and bless his name!
Psalm 100:4 (KJV)

Lord, my soul weeps for the pain You went through.
Yet I am so very grateful for all You came to do.

My heart grieves because of how You bled and died,
With many people shouting and those who cried.

Some mourned Your death but really did not know,
Your life would not end, yet Your blood had to flow.

The Father's plan was done the moment You gave,
For You sacrificed Your perfect life coming to save.

At the Cross You took all our shameful sins away,
When we trust in You, our debt You came to pay.

Lord, how do I thank You for Your blessing to me?
I will praise You forever for setting my soul free.

October 31
THE TRUE MEANING OF LIFE

For we are His workmanship, created in Christ Jesus
for good works, which God prepared beforehand,
that we should walk in them.
Ephesians 2:10 (NKJV)

God, my walk with You is not measured by years,
It is the strength I have gained within the tears.

As I seek You trusting for prayers to come true,
Lord, You know my heart and bring me through.

If my mind overflows with sadness and despair,
Lord, take away those thoughts lingering there.

Our devotion to You is the true meaning to life,
Living in Your will is our assurance from strife.

Lord, I will trust through adversity I must bear,
Yet thank You for love and answers to prayer.

November

November 1
PEACE AND ENDLESS GRACE

How I love Your instruction!
It is my meditation all day long.
Psalm 119:97 (HCSB)

It is in Your presence, Lord; I want to always stay,
As my thoughts are drawn to You by night and day,

While weeping willows sway in whispering wind,
I ponder Your gentle Spirit and hearts You mend.

I see beautiful white clouds in a vast ocean of blue,
Every moment is precious, as I share it with You.

Lord, there is awesome power in Your Holy Name,
And I'm thankful You will always remain the same.

Peace and endless grace are gifts You freely give,
Lord, without You life would be difficult to live.

November 2
MY HUMBLE PRAYER

---

*But he gives greater grace. Therefore he says, "God
resists the proud but gives grace to the humble."
James 4:6 (CSB)*

God, my thoughts struggle as I come to pray,
I find it difficult right now on what to say.

You are so patient waiting timelessly on me,
Yet You know my love is forever with Thee.

I'm only human and make no excuse today,
But so grateful You always guide my way.

I ask for blessings from Your throne above,
For those hurting in this life, I dearly love.

Please give peace for the battles to be won,
And forgive worrying that has been done.

There's many in need of Your healing touch.
And broken hearts that love You so much.

I thank You for hearing my humble prayer.
And praise You, God, for Your faithful care.

November 3
LORD, DRAW ME INTO YOUR ARMS

Be a rock of refuge for me, where I can always go.
Give the command to save me, for You are my rock and fortress.
Psalm 71:3 (HCSB)

Lord, when dreams appear gone You are still here,
It is Your Holy Spirit that comforts our every fear.

Forgive us when the hard journey produces doubt,
When hope seems consumed like a desert drought.

Life can be worrisome for the troubles it will bring,
Yet Your peace comes when to Your hand we cling.

Lord, by faith mountains move when we trust You,
And we are assured You faithfully take us through.

I pray, sweet Lord, draw me into Your arms today.
I will forever praise You for always making a way.

November 4
REFLECTION OF YOUR GRACE

*By whom also we have access by faith into this grace
wherein we stand, and rejoice in hope of the glory of God.
Romans 5:2 (KJV)*

Lord, the past is gone, yet the memories are real.
The hurt is forgiven through Your power to heal.

We are not to judge those things others will do,
But only to believe in the strength found in You.

Lord, shine within me a reflection of Your grace.
Because I know one day, we'll stand face to face.

I will not dwell on the brokenness or the pain,
But thank You for the loss You turned to gain.

Your joy is beyond anything I have ever known.
I praise You, Lord, for the love You have shown.

November 5
HEARTS SET FREE

The Lord does not delay and is not slow about His promise,...
but is patient toward you, not wishing for any to perish
but for all to come to repentance.
2 Peter 3:9 (AMP)

Your glory is to be magnified in Heaven and earth,
And Lord, let all rejoice for Your abundant worth.

You are my Father, with love You filled my heart,
With sincere devotion, I never want to be apart.

I'm happy to be free like the eagle soars up high,
And while creation praises You, Lord, so will I.

Everything I've needed You have already done,
As I gave battles to You, I'm thankful You won.

When I dream of Heaven with its glorious view,
I can only imagine how the angels worship You.

Lord, because of You darkness will always flee,
As strongholds are broken and hearts set free.

November 6
At the Foot of the Cross

*I have written these things to you who believe in the name
of the Son of God, so that you may know that you have eternal life.
1 John 5:13 (HCSB)*

One day, Lord, You will return to claim Your bride.
As we are welcomed with Your arms opened wide.

Your hand holds every breath that only You can do,
Because the beginning and end are planned by You.

Your miracles come as trust births joy from pain,
And tears of gratitude flow down like gentle rain.

As I pray for direction only Your Spirit can give,
I praise You, Lord, for happiness in this life I live.

When hearts break and feeling the sting of loss,
Lord, let them find hope at the foot of the Cross.

The guilt of our past is nothing but a faded scar.
Yet it remains to remind of the journey thus far.

November 7
WHEN ANSWERS AREN'T IN SIGHT

*Jesus answered and said to him, "What I am doing,
you do not realize right now, but you will understand later."
John 13:7 (NASB)*

Lord, we worry when our strength seems to fall.
But You are there every time You hear our call.

Yet we're anxious when answers aren't in sight,
When fear fills our day and every sleepless night.

This life is just a vapor, but our souls rest in You,
You are the One, Lord, who can see us through.

I need You more every moment as years pass by.
For I have learned to trust You and not ask why.

Lord, let me glorify You as I'm led by Your hand,
You are my Rock and on Your Word I will stand.

November 8
GRACE TO ENDURE

May the Lord direct your hearts to God's love
and Christ's endurance.
2 Thessalonians 3:5 (CSB)

Lord, Your Spirit leads from darkness to Your light.
Showing us direction when we have blinded sight.

As I give humble praise, I sing glory to Your name,
Your truth and peace, Lord, I will always proclaim.

In this broken world there is much pain and pride,
Lord, I am sorry because of sin You bled and died.

Life has seasons of change in teaching us Your will,
Yet through many valleys we must learn to be still.

Nothing on this earth compares to Your great love,
Because Your mercy sustains from Heaven above.

Even if uncertain, Lord, help me to walk through.
Grant grace to endure as I keep my eyes on You.

November 9
The Ultimate Act of Love

But God has shown us how much He loves us—
it was while we were still sinners that Christ died for us!
Romans 5:8 (GNT)

Father, I see Your abundant blessings again today,
I am so thankful You watch over me along the way.

I desperately needed Your grace to carry through,
As I searched the journey until at last I found You.

You are my eyes when clouds overshadow sight,
For when vision is weak, I'm guided by Your light.

As I worship I feel Your presence strong and true,
While praising Your name, my peace is made new.

My heart is glad to hear whispers of Your voice.
With each breath, I have many reasons to rejoice.

As You carried the Cross, the ultimate act of love,
You gave mercy from Your perfect throne above.

November 10
My Soul Sings

It is a good and delightful thing to give thanks to the LORD,
to sing praises to Your name, O Most High.
Psalm 92:1 (AMP)

Father, thank You for the nourishment of the rain.
While I walk in the warmth, peace soothes my pain.

You guide me on the journey when I lose my sight,
And Your Spirit comforts through the dark of night.

When trials are difficult, You always direct the way,
Lord, I'm grateful You're with me every single day.

I will praise You, Lord, no matter what life brings.
For deep in my heart lives hope, and my soul sings.

Let me share Your love as others are drawn to You,
To Your Name, Lord, all the glory and honor is due.

November 11
WHEN TRIALS ARE HARD

May the LORD look on you with favor and give you peace.
Numbers 6:26 (GNT)

Lord, please help me make it through this day.
I truly need to hold Your hand along the way.

As I kneel in these moments in humble prayer,
To think of life without You, I could not bear.

While unsure of the future, I have left my past,
My trust is in You, Lord, and will always last.

When trials are hard with no words to express,
Please grant peace apart from daily stress.

Lord, I'll keep my eyes focused totally on You,
For it is Your Spirit that guides me through.

November 12
TRIALS OF THE DAY

---

*Put on the whole armor of God, that you may
be able to stand against the schemes of the devil.
Ephesians 6:11 (ESV)*

Lord, I sense Your whispering to me again today.
I know there's always something You want to say.

You direct my steps on the journey, I don't know.
As I seek Your will wherever You want me to go.

Even if sight is unclear, I know You are with me,
For I'll trust in only You, the future You can see.

In trials of the day and uncertainty of each night,
There I have peace, I'm protected by Your might.

Tomorrow is Yours, yet eternity is by far the best,
For You win every battle, Lord, in You I will rest.

November 13
MY HEART DANCES WITH PRAISE

Therefore I will praise You LORD, among the nations;
I will sing the praises of Your name.
Psalm 18:49 (NIV)

I bow before You as my heart dances with praise,
I will rejoice in You, God, throughout all my days.

Let my spirit shine Your goodness wherever I go,
And Your joy and peace to abundantly over flow.

Your presence gives strength as I walk life's path,
You're my strong refuge from the enemy's wrath.

I am thankful for Your Word growing in my soul.
Because of Your grace, I'm free and made whole.

Lord, let Your eyes see the full depth of my love.
I want to shout my praise to Your throne above.

I'm grateful, God, for the kindness You have done.
But most of all for giving hope through Your Son.

November 14
THROUGH THE TRIAL'S END

"Blessed are those who are persecuted for righteousness'
sake, for theirs is the kingdom of heaven."
Matthew 5:10 (NKJV)

Lord, I find true peace every day I am with You,
For Your tender mercy makes brokenness new.

While my tears flow like an endless rushing tide,
Lord, I know I can run to Your safe arms to hide.

When the testing lingers with no plan in sight,
I will still trust You, Lord, while I hold on tight.

I believe in Your promises and give You my all,
No matter the troubles, whether big or small.

You give me assurance through the trial's end.
And I rejoice, for You are my most loyal friend.

November 15
PROMISE FOR EACH TOMORROW

Cast your burden on the LORD, and he will sustain you;
he will never permit the righteous to be moved.
Psalm 55:22 (RSV)

I lift my eyes to Heaven with sunshine on my face,
To thank You, Lord, for the gift of abundant grace.

You are the perfect peace casting away every fear,
Because life storms are gone when You are near.

You give us hope, a promise for each tomorrow,
You faithfully carry me through trial and sorrow.

You're the one who draws me close in the night.
Telling me to trust and troubles will be all right.

I praise You for Your great and mighty power,
And for Your true love and mercy every hour.

November 16
LET YOUR PEACE BE THE JOURNEY

---

*Now may the Lord of peace Himself continually grant you
peace in every circumstance. The Lord be with you all!*
2 Thessalonians 3:16 (NASB)

I feel Your presence, Lord, faithful and strong,
For each day You have taught my heart a song.

You are my solid refuge and I will dwell there,
Waiting in the quiet as I bow to You in prayer.

Let Your peace be the journey I always seek.
As Your Truth guides me, let Your Spirit speak.

Lord, show my faith to be strong only in You,
For I know Your strength carries me through.

When trials come You comfort till fear is gone,
And in the eye of the storm I will still hold on.

There is never a day I haven't seen Your hand,
I give You praise for my life You have planned.

November 17
Secure Hope

And you will feel secure, because there is hope;
you will look around and take your rest in security.
Job 11:18 (ESV)

Lord, from sunrise to sunset You are always here,
Even in times of testing, I have no reason to fear.

Thank You for strength when I can't walk anymore,
I'm reminded, be strong, good things are in store.

At many a crossroad, I'm uncertain the way to go,
Yet Your steady hand will guide me, this I know.

As the worldly burdens weigh heavy on my mind,
Lord, there is secure hope in You I can surely find.

It is Your love we share that carries me through,
When the days are so weary, Lord, I come to You.

I'm grateful, Lord, in trials as You draw me near.
For You see my life and take care year after year.

November 18
AS I KNEEL IN YOUR PRESENCE

All day long I'll praise and honor you,
O God, for all that you have done for me.
Psalm 71:8 (TLB)

Lord, when I'm weary Your arms of strength gives rest,
You have filled my life with joy and I am truly blessed.

Let my words of gratitude be a pleasure in Your sight.
And Lord, allow everything I do to be humble and right.

I will always give praise for everything You have done,
Honoring only You for all the victories You have won.

As I kneel in Your presence, I desire nearness of You.
Lord, I want to say thank You for bringing me through.

I am truly rich because You are my precious treasure,
To worship You gives my heart the greatest pleasure.

November 19
God of Peace

As for the things you have learned and received and heard and seen in me,
practice these things, and the God of peace will be with you.
Philippians 4:9 (NASB)

Lord, I look back and see all You have done.
The many victories in my life You have won.

There was no way the miracles would ever be,
Yet it is through Your mercy You covered me.

Amid trials Your presence lightens my heart,
Filling the emptiness flowing into every part.

Lord, some days Your will I can't understand.
But I'll trust in everything You have planned.

Let me hear You speak and help me discern,
As I encounter lessons, You want me to learn.

You are my best friend and my God of peace.
For with You, my troubles are sure to cease.

November 20
AT THE FOOT OF YOUR THRONE

*"But blessed is the man who trusts in the Lord
and has made the Lord his hope and confidence."
Jeremiah 17:7 (TLB)*

Lord, I do not understand the testing I'm in.
Yet there is no doubt the battles You will win.

I know You hear every word I humbly pray,
Lord, I need rest and peace through this day.

Your hope gives strength to my weary heart,
And daily, Lord, I feel renewal in every part.

These trials I cannot shoulder all on my own,
So Lord, I lay them at the foot of Your throne.

Out of life's burdens, You'll bring me through.
For divine mercy and hope comes from You.

November 21
IN YOUR LOVING HANDS

Yet, O Lord, You are our Father;
we are the clay, and you our Potter,
and we all are the work of Your hand.
Isaiah 64:8 (AMPC)

Lord, prepare my heart for desires of Your will,
Help me learn while You teach me to be still.

When confusion comes bringing fear and pain,
I can smile because I trust You always reign.

I'll praise You, Lord, through every stormy gale,
For I know Your merciful love will never fail.

You are strength when my faith becomes weak,
And a guiding light while Your Word I seek.

Lord, I give You my all as I wait for Your plans.
I want only a life held in Your loving hands.

November 22
TIMING NEVER TOO LATE

Better is the end of a thing than its beginning,
and the patient in spirit is better than the proud in spirit.
Ecclesiastes 7:8 (ESV)

Lord, every word of praise belongs only to You,
For Your name is worthy where all honor is due.

Your mighty truth reigns over my heart and soul,
For I am a broken vessel You have made whole.

In the midst of the testing I will faithfully trust.
You're my God of grace, so magnificent and just.

Lord, Your timing is never too late in every plea.
For Your goodness and peace always bless me.

Every day of life I want to give praise and glory,
For love is written through Your creation story.

November 23
THROUGH IT ALL

God, who called you to become his child,
will do all this for you, just as he promised.
1 Thessalonians 5:24 (TLB)

Lord, this life is all Yours, please fill it with You,
Show Your desires as I journey my way through.

Let my eyes see Your blessings sent from above,
And let me gain peace from Your precious love.

In times I fail You, please forgive me when I do,
Help me to be thankful with a heart that is true.

As Your hands stretch beyond all limits of time,
You are faithful in valleys and mountains I climb.

There are never battles that are too big or small,
For in every trial, You are faithful through it all.

November 24
PEACE IN THE STORM

---

*But Jesus looked at them and said, "With men it is impossible,
but not with God; for with God all things are possible."
Mark 10:27 (NKJV)*

Lord, mountains are moved by Your powerful love.
For You have granted miracles from Heaven above.

While Your Spirit whispers, You call us to be still,
We must trust Your plan as we wait for Your will.

When fear takes hold, our souls cry out for You,
Your arms hold tightly as we're carried through.

In shadows of doubt, when hope is sadly worn,
Your peace moves in to comfort us in the storm.

Lord, I'm assured by what Your Word has to say,
And I'm so thankful for faithful guidance today.

November 25
By Faith I Will Trust

But whoever keeps His word, truly the love of God is
perfected in him. By this we know that we are in Him.
1 John 2:5 (NKJV)

Lord, I dwell on You as You brighten my day,
With many tears of joy, I come here to pray.

In the silence I hear the song of a small bird,
As I soak in the truth from Your Holy Word.

As nature sings praises, I know You are here,
The beautiful melodies send peace to my ear.

Thank You for every time I've leaned on You,
And trials You faithfully carried me through.

By faith I will trust You as I have in the past,
And I am grateful Your love will always last.

November 26
My Heart Sings Praise

Come, let us sing to the LORD!
Let us shout joyfully to the Rock of our salvation.
Psalm 95:1 (NLT)

Lord, I thank You for Your grace that forgives,
And by Your faithfulness, my soul forever lives.

Please guide and direct as I walk along the way,
Let every word honor You as I go about my day.

Lord, I'll always trust as I journey life through,
Help me be mindful I'm nothing apart from You.

As I pray for strength so my faith will never fail,
I thank You for Your mercy when days are pale.

Lord, in trials without You, I cannot stand strong.
But with You, my heart sings praise all day long.

November 27
In My Sacred Place

In the morning before the sun was up, Jesus went to a place
where He could be alone. He prayed there.
Mark 1:35 (NLV)

Lord, as I praise let Your ears hear a joyful sound,
I think of how I love You and the peace I've found.

In this moment, Lord, I need You here by my side,
You bring a smile to my heart I'll never try to hide.

In Your presence I'll continue to sing with praise,
It's only You, Lord, I want to please all of my days.

You are strength bringing hope to all my dreams,
And the designer of sunlight and flowing streams.

I'll forever be thankful for Your abundant grace.
And for the quiet time shared in my sacred place.

November 28
In the Battles

The Lord will fight for you,
and you shall hold your peace and remain at rest.
Exodus 14:14 (AMPC)

Lord, I trust You for You know what's in store,
When trials overwhelm, I need You even more.

I seek in Your presence to grow closer to You,
For You're my strength and shelter in all I do.

My heart longs to give praise to Your name.
Lord, I'm thankful You are forever the same.

In silence You comfort as tears fall like rain,
And Your arms hold steady, removing pain.

Burdens that come will test my weary soul,
Yet You are the One who makes me whole.

I won't forget the miracles You have done,
For in the battles, Lord, victories You won.

November 29
A Praise Song in All Seasons

Shout joyfully to the LORD, all the earth.
Psalm 100:1 (AMP)

God, You see through the windows of my soul,
Pleasing You is my heart's desire and my goal.

I will patiently wait to hear You gently speak,
You are my only strength whenever I am weak.

Let my life be a praise song in all the seasons,
In happy or sad times for any of Your reasons.

You're always with me when I fall or stumble,
I thank You for grace as I learn to be humble.

There's no comparison to the greatness of You,
For Your peace and mercy, carries me through.

November 30
A Changed Life

"The thief comes only to steal and kill and destroy;
I have come that they may have life, and have it to the full."
John 10:10 (NIV)

Lord, each morning I need to come to You in prayer.
And I know You're listening, You cover me with care.

I thank You as I kneel and praise You for Your plans.
I am a changed life redeemed and held in Your hands.

Lord, through my pain You have birthed a new song,
And in those valleys You have walked with me along.

Sometimes roads are rough and dreams end in tears.
No matter where we go, You always remove our fears.

Lord, with power You can still the raging of the sea.
And with divine grace, You are here to set souls free.

December

December 1
WHEN I SEE YOUR FACE

Let the words of my mouth and the meditation
of my heart be acceptable in your sight,
O LORD, my rock and my redeemer.
Psalm 19:14 (ESV)

Lord, I am so humbled for Your everlasting love.
And thankful you watch over from Heaven above.

Like creation, Lord, I completely depend on You.
For in weakness, I need strength getting through.

Your peace shelters when storms move in strong,
As Your arms carry me when testing lasts so long.

Let my heart grow in beauty found in Your eyes.
While I give You glory, Lord, let Your praises rise.

My trials have been overcome and hurt is healed,
Because You are my strong Rock and my shield.

I love You, Lord, but so unworthy of Your grace.
Yet some day I can rejoice when I see Your face.

December 2
THIS BATTLE ISN'T MINE

And now, Lord, what do I wait for? My hope is in You.
Psalm 39:7 (NLV)

Lord, this battle isn't mine, for it belongs to You.
I will be obedient as You walk with me through.

I know You love me and promise to never leave,
As I remain in Your Word, I will always believe.

When dreams seem hopeless You are still good,
Even through trials I have not yet understood.

As I wait in the quietness, I know You are here,
For dwelling in Your presence takes away fear.

The enemy wants to steal all the peace You give,
But, Lord, I'll praise You through each day I live.

December 3
LORD, PREPARE MY HEART

Those who make themselves clean from all those evil things,
will be used for special purposes, because they are dedicated
and useful to their Master, ready to be used for every good deed.
2 Timothy 2:21 (GNT)

Lord, please guide my journey as only You can,
As I sit here in the quiet waiting for Your plan.

Teach my eyes to capture only what I am to see,
And Lord, let Your divine will be lived out in me.

Lord, prepare my heart to glorify You every day,
Open my ears to hear You speak in every way.

Save me from pride and the enemy's selfish gain.
As Your Spirit dwells within, please take reign.

Lord, You have my heart and You hold the key,
As always, I trust You to hear my humble plea.

December 4
FOR ALL ETERNITY

And this is the testimony: God has given us eternal life,
and this life is in his Son.
1 John 5:11 (NIV)

Lord, I saw a lovely rose reminding me of You,
It was a peaceful image, magnificent and true.

I ponder the sights when we will finally meet,
Will I shout out with joy or praise at Your feet?

To look in Your eyes, what thoughts will I see?
I cherish my dreams of Your arms holding me.

In listening to You, I cling to Your every word,
As I hear melodies of angels, I've never heard.

Your presence will be no other I have known,
As loved ones, glorify You upon Your throne.

I worship You, Lord, for all eternity through.
For my heart and love are promised to You.

December 5
Praise at Each Morning Sun

From the rising of the sun to its setting,
the name of the LORD is to be praised!
Psalm 113:3 (NASB)

As I bow, Lord, I quietly whisper Your name,
There Your sweet presence is always the same.

It is in Your mercy I pray for comfort and rest,
For in Your loving arms, Lord, I'm truly blessed.

There is no one that satisfies my thirsty heart,
For it is Your divine hands that hold every part.

Let my words be humble at each morning sun,
While I praise You for my battles, You have won.

Lord, I'm grateful for over the earth You reign.
Because You're the hope breaking every chain.

Forever I'll honor You, Lord, everyday through,
As Your Spirit guides my way in glorifying You.

December 6
IN GRATEFUL PRAYER

*For everything God has created is good, and nothing is
to be rejected if it is received with gratitude.*
1 Timothy 4:4 (AMP)

Lord, at the ocean I enjoyed the artistry of Your hand.
Blue water and sandy beaches as only You planned.

Seashells with intricate designs beachcombers seek,
All of Your vast creations are beautiful and unique.

I walked in the footprints and my mind was on You,
For in trials, Your arms have carried me through.

As my eyes gazed up to Heaven, so high and so far,
I pondered how Your love has removed every scar.

The vision so peaceful reveals Your mercy and care.
I just want to praise You, Lord, in grateful prayer.

December 7
YOUR VICTORIES I CLAIM

Finally, be strong in the Lord, and in the strength of his might.
Ephesians 6:10 (ASV)

God, You give freely through abundant love,
As my heart is covered by grace from above.

My life has been rescued You came to save,
I sing praises You have risen from the grave.

You birth each day with a new dawn's light,
There's beauty to behold, a wonderful sight.

Your Word is a sword held firm in my hand,
For on Your foundation I will always stand.

Your victories I claim over the enemy's lies,
It is Your beautiful name where praises rise.

As I live each day, take control in every part,
For You are sovereign and reign in my heart.

December 8
LORD, GUIDE MY JOURNEY

For all who are led by the Spirit of God are sons of God.
Romans 8:14 (RSV)

Lord, I see Your goodness in the blue sky.
In all the beauty, I lift Your name on high.

Every breath I take Your mercies are new,
I am so elated because I am loved by You.

Let me hear even a whisper as You speak.
For it is You my heart will eternally seek.

Lord, if clouds come to shadow my view,
Teach me to stay totally centered on You.

As I pray, asking peace within Your plans,
I know You hold my needs in Your hands.

I'll give You honor and glory every day,
Lord, guide my journey as I go Your way.

December 9
As Trials Come

The LORD is my light and my salvation; whom shall I fear?
The LORD is the strength of my life; of whom shall I be afraid?
Psalm 27:1 (KJV)

I am Your child, God, let me feel Your presence today.
I desperately need to hear what Your heart has to say.

You came from Heaven to a world with hate and fear,
Yet with Your gentle hand, You erase each fallen tear.

Every sunrise and sunset displays blessings from You,
As trials come my way, You always bring me through.

In storms, when life's uncertainties seem to close in,
Your Spirit assures me Your power will always win.

Thank You, God, for grace You've granted freely to us,
As we lay down our prayers and give You our trust.

December 10
As I Trust in Your Timing

For everything there is a season, and a time for
every purpose under heaven:
Ecclesiastes 3:1 (ASV)

Lord, when broken tears are finally wiped away,
I'll be with You on that wonderful, glorious day.

While I dwell on earth, I pray for a humble heart,
As my life gives glory to only You in every part.

You are the One who can move the mountain tall,
And in hardened hearts You direct walls to fall.

Your hand brings rain and makes white the snow,
You hold all power, bidding strong winds to blow.

The earth is Yours and all things created within,
You are sovereign, Lord, for all battles You win.

Mercy and goodness comes faithfully from You,
As I trust in Your timing, You bring me through.

December 11
The Eyes of My Heart

*I pray that the eyes of your heart may be enlightened,
so that you will know what is the hope of His calling, what
are the riches of the glory of His inheritance in the saints.*
Ephesians 1:18 (NASB)

Lord, in weakness You have made me strong,
I'm grateful You walk with me all day long.

Your Spirit comforts when upon You I call,
As You provide for my needs, big or small.

In bondage, You remove our every chain.
And I thank You, Lord, for healing the pain.

There is no battle the enemy will ever win,
Because You are my Redeemer over all sin.

Lord, as I seek to follow, teach me to be still,
Allow the eyes of my heart to see Your will.

Help me honor You while I journey through.
For all the praise and glory belongs to You.

December 12
HOW AM I HONORING YOU, LORD?

O Lord my God, I will give thanks to You with all my heart.
I will bring honor to Your name forever.
Psalm 86:12 (NLV)

How am I honoring You, Lord? I ponder this today,
Let my ears hear Your words of what it is You say.

My heart is filled with happiness, a joy forever new.
I will walk in peace, yet often You carry me through.

Thank You, Lord, for Your goodness You freely give,
My love grows more each day You allow me to live.

Your grace is abundant but nothing at all I deserve,
Please teach me how to honor for it is You I serve.

Let me never forget how You have richly blessed,
I am thankful I can come to You when I need rest.

December 13
A Name I Love

And there is salvation in no one else;
for there is no other name under heaven that has been
given among people by which we must be saved
[for God has provided the world no alternative for salvation]."
Acts 4:12 (AMP)

Jesus, Your name is strong yet so sweet.
A name I love and some day I will meet.

Your name is above all we will ever need,
It is a name that removes sin and greed.

Your name gives peace when on my knees,
Reaching far beyond vast oceans and seas.

Lord, Your name is comfort in life's stress.
Thank You for salvation as souls say yes.

Your name is freedom, You freely forgive,
Through Your saving grace, we can live.

Your name is holy, redeeming as we pray,
Lord, we need You, draw us close today.

December 14
MY PRINCE OF PEACE

Peace I leave with you. My peace I give to you.
I do not give to you as the world gives.
Don't let your heart be troubled or fearful.
John 14:27 (CSB)

In the quiet, Lord, I know You always care.
As I share with You in this evening prayer.

Within my heart, Lord, You faithfully reign,
I am so thankful Your mercy comforts pain.

I wait for Your voice in the beauty by night.
Even in darkness, Your light shines bright.

I lay my concerns humbly into Your hands.
Because I know, Lord, it's all in Your plans.

In life storms You tell raging winds to cease,
So powerful, yet You are my Prince of Peace.

December 15
IN YOUR FAITHFULNESS

But it is good for me to be near God;
I have put my trust in the Lord God and made Him
my refuge, that I may tell of all Your works.
Psalm 73:28 (AMPC)

Lord, give me strength as I walk the journey through.
And in fires of adversity, keep my eyes fixed on You.

Whenever I feel anxious, You give comfort and peace,
In Your faithfulness, Lord, my troubles always cease.

All my life I have needed You that's been clear to see,
Lord, every time I've cried, You've been here for me.

When my soul is tired, You remind me to remain still,
For You are my refuge as I strive to live in Your will.

Let Your Spirit flow through so only Your love shines.
To glorify You in Your plan and only by Your designs.

December 16
ENDURING GRACE

*For the grace of God has appeared, bringing
salvation for all people.*
Titus 2:11 (CSB)

God, there is no way on this journey without You,
It is only by Your strength I can make it through.

Your Holy Spirit sustains me with relentless love,
For You, Lord, are my Father, guiding from above.

Days come and days go yet You are always here,
No matter the trials, Your hands wipe every tear.

Your gentle peace calms in the darkest of night,
Because Your presence reveals Your divine light.

As my thoughts envision a picture of Your face,
Lord, my heart is so grateful for enduring grace.

Only You deserve the honor and greatest glory,
For to You I am thankful for Your divine story.

December 17
No Key Needed

If you confess with your mouth, "Jesus is Lord",
and believe in your heart that God raised Him
from the dead, you will be saved.
Romans 10:9 (CSB)

Lord, Your Word tells of a future You've planned.
When we believe trusting our heart to Your hand.

Your magnificent Heaven will be an awesome place,
As glorious light illuminates from Your loving face.

The marvelous city gates will never be closed to us,
And no key needed, for there is only love and trust.

As written, Heaven's streets are made of pure gold,
For through grace Your plan will someday unfold.

There will be no more tears, sorrow or earthly pain,
Only joy unimaginable will be ours as eternal gain.

December 18
RAINBOWS AMID THE STORM

*Honor and thanks be to the Lord, who carries our heavy loads
day by day. He is the God who saves us.*
Psalms 68:19 (NLV)

Lord, so many times I've trusted what I couldn't see,
But I remember the words, "Don't worry, follow me."

You painted rainbows as I've walked amid the storm,
For in Your arms I rested while hope kept me warm.

My faith rests in You, for in my strength I cannot do,
As You have shown, You'll always carry me through.

Lord, Your presence will forever be the One I seek,
For You comfort when my spirit becomes so weak.

I thank You for Your sacrifice and Your shed blood.
Your saving grace cleansed me like a mighty flood.

When someone asks, "How do I know this is true?"
I can say truly my peace and joy remains in You.

December 19
BOUNDLESS GRACE

LORD, be gracious to us; we long for you.
Be our strength every morning, our salvation in time of distress.
Isaiah 33:2 (NIV)

Lord, You're my hope and my constant stay.
As You guide on the path of the unseen way.

You know the future it is held in Your hand,
Firmly on Your name, Lord, I'll always stand.

If trials are burdensome and seem too hard,
It is You that comforts, my heart You guard.

As I live for You it gives my soul such peace,
I'm glad to know Your love will never cease.

I sing praise because You're always with me,
For in boundless grace, I'm eternally set free.

December 20
A Mighty Tower

*I have been crucified with Christ: and I myself no longer
live, but Christ lives in me. And the real life I now have within
this body is a result of my trusting in the Son of God,
who loved me and gave himself for me.*
Galatians 2:20 (TLB)

Lord, I need to receive from Your heart today.
Please let me hear every word You have to say.

Thank You for comfort as trials become great,
For I know, Lord, Your timing is never too late.

Your sweet Spirit's voice is all I desire to seek,
As I kneel in prayer, help me hear You speak.

In You there is hope and promised assurance,
For You give strength and heavenly endurance.

You are faithful to me even in the darkest hour,
Because You are steadfast, like a mighty tower.

December 21
Through Your Grace

And we have known and believed the love
that God has for us. God is love, and he who abides
in love abides in God, and God in him.
1 John 4:16 (NKJV)

Lord, I know there is strength in Your hands.
And I believe life is designed by divine plans.

When difficult trials come to steal joy away,
I trust You, Lord, in Your promises as I pray.

Lord, it's only because of You I can truly cope,
For Your Spirit brings sweet peace and hope.

Your Word comforts me throughout the day,
You're my bright light guiding journey's way.

I'll praise You, Lord, Your faithfulness is clear,
With You beside me, there's no room for fear.

I thank You for giving Your life for mankind,
For it's through Your grace true love we find.

December 22
My Sacred Place

Those who live in the shelter of the Most High
will find rest in the shadow of the Almighty.
Psalm 91:1 (NLT)

Lord, my sacred place I find in the silence with You,
As trials overwhelm, it's there You take me through.

It is where I share my heart and no one else hears,
It is there You cradle me while wiping away fears.

In this place, Your joy comforts me all the day long,
It is there You bless my heart with a beautiful song.

In my special place, You love me and forgive my sin,
Where Your grace is real and the victories You win.

It is my sacred place I go and never want to leave,
It is there Your name is exalted and peace I receive.

December 23
SACRIFICIAL LOVE

And to know the love of Christ which surpasses knowledge,
that you may be filled with all the fullness of God.
Ephesians 3:19 (RSV)

Lord, I want my life to bring You honor and glory,
To tell of Your sacrificial love and beautiful story.

Nothing can separate me from Your loving arms,
And in Your power You shield all hurt and harms.

The troubles that burden, You always work out.
I will trust You, for there is no reason for doubt.

Lord, I'm thankful You always carry me through.
Even though I don't deserve divine love so true.

All Your plans of tomorrow I do not understand,
Yet I know You're here holding tight to my hand.

December 24
PRAISES WITH ENDLESS SONG

The LORD protects and defends me; I trust in him. He gives me help and makes me glad; I praise him with joyful songs.
Psalm 28:7 (GNT)

Lord Jesus, be my feet as I walk in Your ways,
Take my hand and lead throughout my days.

Help me feel Your strength when I am weak,
For it is only You, my Lord, I will always seek.

Let my ears hear Your voice whispering to me,
And my eyes discern what You want me to see.

It is the wings of peace that shelter my head,
For You are my refuge and sustaining bread.

Every day and night for Your presence I long,
While I sing Your praises with endless song.

December 25
YOU CAME WITH A MESSAGE

For I have come down from heaven, not to do My
will, but the will of Him who sent me.
John 6:38 (HCSB)

Lord, in every sunrise my thoughts go to You.
My heart is thankful for the blessings You do.

In love, Your grace and mercy You freely give,
As You came with a message in this life we live.

Your hand reaches to those who do not know,
To give eternal life yet Your blood had to flow.

In broken vessels Your light will shine through,
As they surrender their emptiness up to You.

I praise You, Lord, for You are perfect and just.
In humbled prayer I bow, I give You my trust.

December 26
ALONG EVERY PATHWAY

"Call on Me in a day of trouble;
I will rescue you, and you will honor Me."
Psalm 50:15 (HCSB)

Lord, I take all that I am laying it at Your feet,
As I seek Your presence, my heart is complete.

In valleys my joy has been lifted by Your hand,
It was there You held me when I couldn't stand.

I praise You for everything that You have done,
For the many battles, You have faithfully won.

With love You have always been gracious to me,
As I walked through trials, only You could see.

Along every pathway and on each winding road,
You came to rescue while You carried my load.

Forever You are cherished as my truest friend,
No matter the struggle in Your time, You mend.

December 27
When the End I Can't See

I know, LORD, that our lives are not our own.
We are not able to plan our own course.
Jeremiah 10:23 (NLT)

God, in this valley I haven't heard Your voice,
Trials are difficult when I don't see a choice.

In looking through my tears I know You care,
As I bow before You in broken, humble prayer.

Even though You're silent, I know You're near,
I will trust even when answers are not clear.

If Your word is "no" I promise to understand,
For it's all in Your will as You have planned.

Your delays I've found draw me closer to You,
For in Your testing, hope carries me through.

Even in the darkness when the end I can't see,
As I call Your name, Your Spirit comforts me.

December 28
GREATEST WORTH

Great is the LORD! He is most worthy of praise!
No one can measure his greatness
Psalm 145:3 (NLT)

Lord, I bow humbly lifting Your name on high,
Through every teardrop, Your hand wipes dry.

I speak Your praises for another beautiful day,
Lord, You know my thoughts as I come to pray.

I'll follow Your ways as Your Holy Spirit leads,
For You are my guide providing all my needs.

As Your light flows through me in joyful peace,
I am thankful in Your presence worries cease.

Lord, I give all of me, draw in every single part.
Let Your sweet Spirit consume filling my heart.

My Savior, You are exalted above all the earth,
You are King of all; You are of greatest worth.

December 29
My Shelter

As for God, His way is perfect;
The word of the LORD is proven;
He is a shield to all who trust in Him.
Psalm 18:30 (NKJV)

Dear Lord, I am Your child please draw me near,
At Your feet I will lay all my trials and every fear.

You are great with amazing love, deep and true.
For in You I trust, no other can compare to You.

You set a foundation for my faith to firmly stand.
As I wait one day to see all You divinely planned.

Your ways are perfect and Your promises sure,
Lord, You are my shelter with You I am secure.

I lift my eyes to Heaven seeking Your holy face,
While I come to You, Lord, in this sacred place.

December 30
PROMISE OF HOPE

---

*This hope will not disappoint us, because God's love
has been poured out in our hearts through the Holy Spirit
who was given to us.*
Romans 5:5 (HCSB)

Lord, whenever life is uncertain truth in You I find.
In seasons of testing, You know my heart and mind.

When days seem bleak, I know You will always care,
For Your Spirit reminds me You are faithfully there.

Lord, even when Your answers I cannot see or hear,
No matter the trial, I'll have faith that You are near.

In our brokenness, Your sweet grace dries every eye,
Then after the storm, You place rainbows in the sky.

Our promise of hope flows from Your precious name.
Because Your endless love remains forever the same.

December 31
Thankful for Grace

I will bless the LORD at all times;
His praise shall continually be in my mouth.
Psalm 34:1 (KJV)

I love You, Lord, much more than I can say.
Close to You always is where I want to stay.

No matter what this life may bring or hold,
Your presence is worth far more than gold.

Keep my eyes always focused solely on You,
And my heart humbly and truly devoted, too.

You deserve my praise faithfully every day,
For protection, You give walking on my way.

I will worship You for Your everlasting love,
And for all Your mercies granted from above.

Lord, I'm thankful for grace I do not deserve,
In my heart, You're the treasured One I serve.

CPSIA information can be obtained
at www.ICGtesting.com
Printed in the USA
JSHW010150040421
13210JS00003B/7